Thoughts

ON PEOPLE, PLANET, & PROFIT

AMY DOMINI

Thoughts

ON PEOPLE, PLANET, & PROFIT

With special thanks to Jurriaan Kamp for
giving me the opportunity to share my thoughts
through these columns over the years.

ORDERING INFORMATION
Special discounts are available on quantity purchases
by corporations, associations, and others, as well as for
college textbook/course adoption use. For details, contact
Domini Impact Investments at the e-mail address above.

Library of Congress Cataloging-in-Publication Data
ISBN: 978-1-7377091-3-8

FOR MIKE, MAGGIE, ENZO, AND
THE LITTLE GIRLS OF TOMORROW

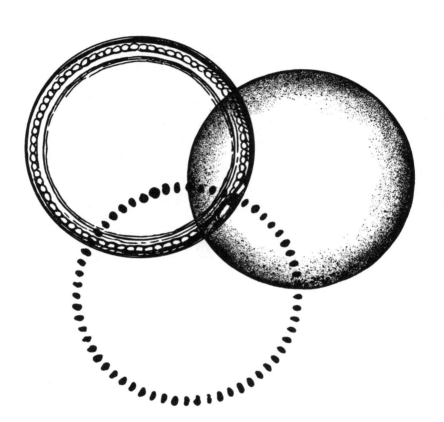

⭕ People

⭕ Planet

Profit

"...it all begins with
seeing simple truths."

Thirty years ago, I found my passion for investing with purpose – a positive purpose for our future. From that day forward I have dedicated myself to spreading the word: if we are to live on a green planet and if we are to allow every human to thrive, investors must play an active role. The future I envisioned for my grandchildren could not come about without investing in it. And so, it became my mission to convince investors to join me, to guide dollars into the creation of that vision.

Through providing standards for research, supporting academic research, and bringing together networks of advocates for investors who care, I played a role in every stage of this concept and nurtured it until impact investing was a field. Slowly, the numbers have proved me—and moved me. In 2020, according to The Forum for Sustainable and Responsible Investment (US SIF), 33 percent of the $51.4 trillion in total U.S. assets under professional management were invested in sustainable, responsible, and impact investing strategies. Today, many view impact investing as a growing trend. But for me, it will always be a proud tradition.

To celebrate the anniversary of my impact investing journey, I have chosen to share this collection of columns. My hope in writing these is to express in simple terms what the collective action of caring investors could make possible. Written between 2007 and 2016, the collection is sorted into three sections: People, Planet, and Profit. The triple P bottom line is widely acknowledged to be the purpose of responsible investors worldwide.

When I first thought of creating a vehicle that individual investors could use as a means of joining together to define what is right and ethical, such thinking was considered both revolutionary and naive. Investing, it was argued, is innately amoral. Investors do what they do and government or society does what it does, the argument went.

That seemed illogical to me. Any thinking person could see that investors would always push for profit and that profit would be most easily gained by stealing from the commons, from our natural ecosystem, and indeed, from our more vulnerable citizens. Further, any rational person could understand that investors are also people, and that their human nature should desire a verdant planet occupied by peaceful and fulfilled people. Finally, financial investments are massive and coordinated globally. It was only logical that they be utilized to help humankind to achieve its utmost potential.

Of course, if we wanted to, we could focus on what's discouraging. Over the past thirty years we've witnessed environmental destruction, the growth of inconceivable wealth and income gaps, and petty wars fought with horrific weaponry. But despite this distressing backdrop, an ever persistent set of investor voices has channeled their dollars positively and pushed for better, knowing that money talks, even in optimistic ways.

When we launched our first mutual fund, the majority in South Africa had no vote. That came about three years later. Corporate social responsibility reports, chief sustainability officers, research houses dedicated to environmental, social, and governance discovery, stock exchanges mandating the disclosure of the same as a qualification for listing, academic careers in business schools for positively impacting our lives—none of this existed. All of it came into being as the result of our investors, and those like them, joining together to help define what is best for us all, joining together to make it possible.

Domini Impact Investments LLC is a small asset manager amongst financial giants. But we have played a key role in legitimizing and advocating for people who believe that caring investors are essential to achieving ecological sustainability and universal human dignity. I am a fortunate woman. I can look back on the work of the firm I helped to create and truly say that we have made a difference. But it all begins with seeing simple truths. It begins with the collective realization that the secret to making an impact is small. Together, we can each do something—and this, in the end, is everything.

People

Money makes the world go round

*M*any people understand that when you're buying food, price is not the only consideration. It's also important to think about the additives and pesticides you're putting into your body, whether certain kinds of fish are being driven to extinction, and how the people who grow your vegetables are being treated.

People are beginning to ask similar kinds of questions about their investments. By putting their money into the stocks of certain companies, and then pressing those companies to do the right thing, investors are starting to create change. Being a conscious investor is a lot like being a conscious shopper.

Once people realize certain options are open to them, they start down paths that can transform their lives. For instance, one of my local supermarkets specializes in healthy and organic food. I was first attracted to it because of the wide selection of fresh fish, beautifully displayed on crushed ice. Returning frequently to the store, I started paying attention not only to whether the fish looked and smelled good, but whether they were caught in the wild or farm-raised using organic methods. Eventually I started seeking out fish that were caught or raised locally. The choices the store offered actually turned me into a more conscious shopper.

Something similar happened to me years ago when I was working as a stockbroker. The financial industry often assumes that investors care about nothing but making money, but as I got to know my clients I realized there was more to them than that. They cared about a lot of things—the forests and birds, issues of war and peace, their children's health—in addition to making money. So when I was asked to recommend a company that was on the verge of getting a big military contract, I realized I didn't want to ask the compassionate people who were my clients to invest in killing machines.

Like many important ideas, this one was pretty simple: The way you invest your money matters. If you're a doctor or care about health issues, it makes no sense to invest in tobacco companies. If you're a birdwatcher, it makes no sense to invest in pesticide manufacturers that kill birds. That's when I really started connecting the dots. It became obvious to me that we should invest our dollars according to the same values that we use to live our lives.

One recent example brings us back to the supermarket. The families of coffee growers were going hungry in many countries because the prices the growers received for their crops in the world market no longer covered their expenses in growing the coffee. After dialogue with Procter & Gamble, one of the companies in which my socially responsible fund invests, the company agreed to begin buying fair trade coffee, which guarantees the growers a minimum price per pound. It's now one of the major U.S. buyers. Of course, conscious shoppers who seek out fair trade products create the demand for this coffee and play an important role in supporting smallholder coffee growers throughout the world.

As we sometimes say, money makes the world go round. A conscious approach to shopping and investing can profoundly affect the way that it turns.

*W*aking the sleeping giant

---- ❖ ----

In 1929, when the U.S. stock market crashed, less than 10 percent of American families owned stock. Today, despite the increasing gap between rich and poor, roughly 50 percent of American families are stockholders. In Europe, and around the world as well, stock ownership is being democratized. Millions of ordinary people are now "in the market." But relatively few of those new stockholders actually own company shares directly. Far more invest through intermediaries. They may invest in mutual funds, or their employers may invest in pension funds on their behalf.

In all these cases, an individual's money becomes part of a vast pool of assets, made up of mutual funds, pension funds, public endowments, ETFs, or unit trusts. In a similar way, non-profit organizations pool small donations from thousands of individual donors and invest them in charitable trusts, foundation funds, and university endowments.

The institutional investors that regulate these asset pools are giants, controlling assets that range from hundreds of millions to many billions of dollars. Regular people own the assets, but institutions do the investing.

Meanwhile, the financial markets have been changing in other ways—notably by becoming single-mindedly focused on short-term profit. Risk has been redefined as little more than the risk of missing next quarter's earnings. But in the pursuit of near-term profits, corporations overlook many types of risk that don't appear on an income statement: risks of corporations exploiting their workers, poisoning the land and water, contributing to climate change, and producing unsafe products.

Many enlightened investors have come to understand these risks, and have elected to invest in a way that takes justice, sustainability, and the well-being of future generations into account. But there is a sleeping giant in all of this, one that can drive change on a much larger scale. That sleeping giant is the institutional investor.

Institutions typically invest on such a large scale that they must diversify broadly. They own such a dizzying variety of securities—virtually everything, in fact—that the largest have come to be called "universal" investors. They are generally designed to be permanent, self-perpetuating institutions, so it makes little sense for them to focus, as the market's dominant culture dictates, on the short-term profits of individual companies.

Owning everything, and investing on a very long-term horizon, gives the idea that institutions should be thinking about the overall economic health and well-being of the society in which they're invested—because that's what they really own.

Some institutional investors have begun to recognize this broader set of responsibilities and risks. Initiatives like the Institutional Investors Group on Climate Change, representing assets of nearly $4 trillion, and the UN's Principles for Responsible Investment—with signatories representing assets of more than $10 trillion—show that institutions are beginning to take environmental and social factors seriously in their investment decisions. They're becoming more active participants in the companies they own.

The sleeping giant is beginning to stir, but we must wake him up and put him to work. The vast sums controlled by institutional investors are ours, and their great power should also be ours. It is up to us to tell these monoliths that we care about our well-being and about the future as much as about our wealth. We need to tell them to send this message to the companies we own.

It's getting late, there's much to be done, and we can't afford to let that giant stay in bed all day.

Not everything that counts can be counted

For some years now, I've been collecting early 20th-century photographs of street scenes in Naples, Italy, where my father was born. The images portray the minutiae of daily life: Women and children selling goods or playing in the streets and men displaying the catches they made at sea. When I gaze at these images, I'm always surprised by how similar the standard of living depicted therein seems to the one I see in photographs from the same era in America: The children are well fed, their feet are shod, they wear caps to protect their faces from the sun. There's no litter on the streets and the buildings and roads seem to be in a good state of repair.

Then I traveled to other countries. In Pondicherry (India), Bangkok, Panama City, Lima, and Havana, I saw similar pictures. During the 1920s, people around the world seemed to be at about the same spot, from a social development point of view. The cities show a mix of horses with wagons and early automobiles along with light rail and bicycles. Buildings and large public parks line the water's edge to look toward the water with large public piazzas or parks before them. Sometimes, you find pictures of students in classrooms lined up with their teachers. These pictures look very much alike.

This morning, I searched the Internet for pictures of Cairo, Rio de Janeiro, Johannesburg, and Addis Ababa. It was the same in each of these cities as it was in Naples: well-fed children, street vendors in gay moods, solid buildings lining parks or waterways, and almost everyone in shoes. So, what happened? How could so many of these once-great cities of the world have fallen into such disrepair? What global scourge hit the southern hemisphere so much harder than the northern? How did we go from a time when societies the world over were traveling along their paths at roughly the same pace, at least insofar as is revealed in old city photographs, to the disparities we see today?

It's hard not to blame the development of multinational corporations. Certainly, we can look at corruption, population growth, and transportation issues, but in the end, one has to acknowledge that some local, vibrant, even charming societies have been turned into horrifying masses of misery while others have thrived. As far as culprits are concerned, I'm not the first to suspect world trade, driven by corporate demands. In 2005, the international development charity Christian Aid published a report on the costs of free trade. The group estimated that Malawi, for instance, would have had a gross domestic product 8 percent higher after liberalization had it not opened itself up to cheap imports.

The truth is that people need production, not simply consumption, to maintain a functioning economy. In 1994, the World Trade Organization offered Haiti protection (the country had been in the hands of the military for three years and was re-entering democracy) in exchange for greatly reduced trading tariffs.

Agricultural companies wanted to sell their goods to the people of the Caribbean Cheap rice and chicken parts flooded Haiti, and the indigenous agricultural businesses folded. Poverty rates rose, and joblessness and hopelessness became pervasive. The case is widely used for study, but the extrapolation is not. Using multinational companies as the sole means of achieving economic well-being is a failed model. The North is robbing the South of hope.

Realistically, we're not going to do away with multinationals, but we can hold them more accountable. We can demand that they take increasing ownership of the problems they create. On a very small scale, this is happening. Domini Impact Investments recently helped convince the steel company Nucor that it could reduce human misery, even slavery, by being more careful about how it bought raw materials.

Responsible investors have dozens, perhaps hundreds, of small victories to share, but it's like fighting a mudslide. Global forces are so very strong. The possibility of Addis Ababa and Lima resembling New York or London during my lifetime is slim. Nonetheless, it's essential to keep trying. Bringing hope and dignity to 1,000 or 100,000 people may not save the planet, but it counts.

Strengthening the weakest link

Over the course of several weeks last spring, pet owners in the U.S. noticed their cats and dogs were falling sick. A toy poodle named Jasmine died of kidney failure in Easton, Maryland. A cat named Brutus died in San Clemente, California. Carrie, a cairn terrier at a shelter in Kansas City, Kansas, went into convulsions but survived after $1,000 of veterinary care. Gradually it became clear that these animals had all eaten pet food containing wheat gluten contaminated with the industrial chemical melamine, which may have been added because it can make food appear to have more protein than it actually has. The gluten was traced to a supplier in China.

At the same time, other problems were arising with Chinese imports. Toys were found to be coated with lead paint. Imported monkfish was found to be toxic pufferfish. Some 51 people were killed in Panama by cold medicine containing a toxic substitute for glycerin. Lawsuits drew attention to children harmed by swallowing magnets from Chinese toys, including a 20-month-old boy who died on Thanksgiving in 2005.

In a globalized world, the quality and safety of the products we get often depend on long and complex supply chains. But the supply chain is only as strong as its weakest link.

Even if your investment portfolio is small, by choosing to invest your money with managers who are committed to making the world better, you can help strengthen the safety of the supply chain. Here's how:

Research the retailers.

Many big retailers no longer make their own products, buying them instead in the global marketplace. Actual production is outsourced to contractors in the developing world. By asking the right questions, investors can uncover many of the positive and negative influences these companies and their suppliers have. But more importantly, when Wall Street asks for better behavior, retailers are willing to deliver it.

Press for transparency.

Thanks in part to the work of concerned investors, thousands of companies worldwide are publishing corporate social responsibility reports that lay out their codes of conduct, describe their progress on various issues, and reveal the origins, sources, and producers of their products. Such transparency makes it possible for human rights and environmental organizations to dig deeper, and can lead the way to improvement. It's a business truism that what's reported gets measured, and what's measured gets managed.

Consider people, not just products.

Companies that mistreat workers are more likely to neglect product safety and the environment. When lead paint and other toxic substances are used in products, they are hazardous to the workers as well as the consumers. As investors, we should be concerned not only for our children but for these workers and their families overseas. We should urge the investigation of sweatshop conditions at factories that supply major retailers, and push for greater openness.

Investors, like consumers and regulators, must encourage company executives to know their supply chains and hold their suppliers fully accountable. After all, within the fine web of this globalized economy of ours—in which so much of our food, clothing, medicine, and everything else is manufactured in distant, unknown factories—our lives, and the lives of workers around the globe, depend on the weakest link.

"The supply chain is only as strong as its weakest link."

"Now I'm becoming the oddball."

People, planet, purchasing power

I hate to date myself, but I'm old enough to remember having three pairs of shoes. The Buster Browns were for all the time; these sturdy brown lace-ups were for school, play, and most other activities. Next in usefulness were the black patent leathers with the velvet bow; these were for birthday parties, church, dinner with my grandparents, and holidays. Finally came the Keds. Keds were only for playing tennis. Yes, this is true, and although it was a long time ago, it was in my lifetime.

This would never work today. Possessions have swamped us. Shoes have become specialized; so have scissors, batteries, candles, and razors. Most observers agree that the demand for stuff has horrific implications. It creates ghastly environmental effects as we rip out raw materials to make things. It bankrupts families.

In *Culture and Consumption*, Canadian cultural anthropologist Grant McCracken introduced the concept of the Diderot Effect, the unintentional transformation a simple acquisition sets in motion. In *Regrets on Parting with My Old Dressing Gown*, French Enlightenment philosopher Denis Diderot bemoaned the sorry state of his life, which was the result of a gift of an elegant red dressing gown from a well-meaning friend. The dressing gown had been so fine that he had replaced his straw chair with one covered in Moroccan leather. He had replaced his prints along with his desk and updated his study. This improvement process went on until one day he felt unwelcome in his own study. He had become a slave to a level of fashion that befitted his new dressing gown and regretted it.

It may seem a silly story, but we sense its rightness. And I would argue it gives us a special insight. Perhaps some types of consumption are positive change agents.

Consumption is an enormously influential force. It affects behavior patterns of individuals at the personal level in such a way that whole societies are transformed. When anthropologists attempt to open communications with a jungle tribe, they leave pots and other goods the tribe finds useful and values. The door is opened.

❧ We know this. Now we must harness it. ❧

I look at my own consumption. A sneaky change took place over the past decade. Maybe it started with purchasing Ben & Jerry's yummy ice cream. I found I read the carton and wondered why other ice creams didn't tell me what a fine person I am. Then came Stonyfield's yogurt. I got so educated that I wandered into a Whole Foods. After three visits, I gave up on fruits and vegetables if they weren't organic.

Pretty soon, I was getting political about this. I boycotted coffee shops that didn't offer fair trade coffee; I started reading more and more about the polities of hunger and the dangers of pesticides. I noticed which politicians were raising my issues. It changed me. My eccentric Aunt Sylvia doesn't buy any clothing first hand. She's in her eighties and has saved what is rumored throughout the family to be a fortune. But she thinks buying new clothing is just plain wasteful. I've gone from thinking she was an oddball to thinking she's fantastic.

Now I'm becoming the oddball. When plastic bags come from a dry cleaner, I tie off the opening where the hanger was and use them as garbage bags. Last Christmas, my adult children came over to take the ribbons, boxes, papers, and cards I'd saved, sometimes for several years running. It's a lucky thing they did, because I gave up physical gifts four years ago so have no use for the trimmings. It isn't that I'm against giving. I put three dollar bills in my pocket each morning and give them to the first three people who ask.

Did buying Ben & Jerry's ice cream make me a more tolerant woman? It did mark the beginning of a change. Like Diderot, I'm caught in a continuous process of expanding and improving my new sense of self. But unlike Diderot, it feels right. I feel more and more welcome. I feel more and more a part of something important and good.

I'm hoping the purchase of mutual fund shares from a responsible fund family does the same thing. The investor has taken a casual, perhaps thoughtless step, little suspecting he or she has begun a journey of personal redefinition. At some level, this person is no longer one of the overwhelmed, buffeted by forces beyond his or her control. This individual will take small steps: shop more deliberately, vote more deliberately, read the newspapers differently, and be a more engaged (and tolerant) citizen.

No more business as usual

As I write this month's column, the primary election cycle here in the U.S. is in full swing. By the time you read this, the identity of our Democratic presidential candidate may well be known, but right now it's anybody's guess. What has become crystal clear, however, is that the American people are focused on something that's being called "change."

With the military mired in a brutal war and the economy apparently entering a recession, it's easy to see why the banner of change has become popular. And perhaps unsurprisingly, the banner is being raised by candidates not only from the opposition party but from the party in power.

Its meaning, however, isn't exactly clear or consistent. To some, change means little more than a different face with the same policies. To others, it represents real changes in direction—withdrawal from Iraq, and universal health insurance. Some candidates go still further.

If you look at the opinion polls and listen to the messages of change that are resonating with the public, all of this appears to signify a deepening uneasiness with the shape of the political and economic system.

Candidates—at least those on the Democratic side of the election, which is where much of the energy seems to be—are competing as to who has more effectively and completely rejected the campaign contributions of corporations and their lobbyists. They rail against big corporations that ship company profits to overseas tax havens; each candidate claims he or she is the one who can overcome the resistance of pharmaceutical and insurance companies to real healthcare reform;

each one talks about the big military contractors and their impact on U.S. foreign (i.e., war) policy, and about the pressing need for the energy and utility sectors to put a genuine focus on developing energy alternatives at last.

What does this have to do with the usual theme of this column, socially responsible investing? As it turns out, quite a lot.

First, as social investors, we've been talking for a great many years about the issues of corporate behavior and its impact that are being aired during this campaign. In our research, we look closely at how companies use (or abuse) their political influence, at the gigantic social costs of for-profit healthcare, at the dangerous influence of private military contractors on the conduct of war and foreign policy, at companies' responses to climate change, and at the impact of government contracts and tax incentives on corporate strategies. We set standards for corporate behavior and use them to guide us in selecting our investments. And we tell companies that these issues matter to their owners.

Second, and of equal importance, let's remember that the people who speak to us through opinion polls—the people being energized by messages of real change— aren't just voters and citizens; many are investors as well. As they respond to political messages about a broken system and the effect of corporate activities on that system, they'll come to understand that their investments can have a real impact. When investors send companies a "business as usual" message—which is what they do when they invest in the conventional way—what they get is business as usual, and our society and planet just can't afford more of that. So, they're starting to send companies a different message—a message about fairness, sustainability, and change. They invest for their own financial goals, while funding the world they want their children to inherit.

cMaking slavery history

As a responsible investor, I like to think about how I can use the power of my investments to create a better future. I look for opportunities to invest in companies that are rolling out energy-saving engines, building lower-cost solar cells, selling healthy organic food. But while I'm looking to the future, I can't forget that some of the ugliest aspects of the past are still with us.

My investment firm has focused, over many years, on improving conditions for workers around the world. Together with non-governmental organizations and investor coalitions, we've encouraged corporations to take responsibility for conditions in the mines, farms, and factories where they source their products and to ensure that workers are covered by basic standards concerning safety, working hours, and pay. In the course of this work, we've seen some truly terrible things.

We don't often use the word "slavery." But in fact, many industries benefit from it. The awful truth is that slavery doesn't exist only in history books. It's a global phenomenon. Most recently, scrutiny has turned to Latin America, where nearly 1 million people are used as forced, unpaid labor.

Slaves in Brazil labor in logging camps and gold mines to make charcoal. They're recruited from poor areas of the country and transported to remote regions to work for low or no wages. Isolation, lack of money, and the regular threat of violence prevent them from escaping. They live and work in brutal and unsanitary conditions, all the time suffering from heat, malaria, and intestinal parasites.
Investors have an important role to play in ending these abuses. When slaves make charcoal in Brazil, much of that charcoal is used in blast furnaces to produce pig

iron. And much of that pig iron is exported to the major industrialized economies, where it's used to make steel. That steel goes into cars, washing machines, and a thousand other everyday items. That means in a globalized economy, the companies we own may be producing and selling products that have slave labor baked right into them.

The auto, appliance, and steel companies most certainly wish this wasn't so. They didn't, after all, intentionally go out in search of slave-produced raw materials. And, they may ask, can a huge global company really be expected to take responsibility for problems that are so many steps removed from its directly controlled operations—for the production of the fuel that fires the ovens that make the iron that goes into the steel that's used to produce their products?

─────── ● ───────

Our answer is yes. Their products can and should be traced back to the most remote reaches of the supply chain, where relentless pressure to cut costs (so the end product can be sold at the most competitive price) has led to abusive treatment of workers.

It's too soon to know how the story of the charcoal slaves in the Brazilian Amazon will play out, but we're hopeful. It's a fairly straightforward economic rule that when big corporations are no longer willing to purchase materials produced by slaves, the workers in that industry will no longer be enslaved.

The secret is in the sauce

As the daughter of a Neapolitan, I grew up eating pasta with marinara sauce. My father didn't always make it from scratch, but he did so often enough for me to follow his recipe from memory.

Fresh tomatoes were not always available, but we canned them so we had the base for the red sauce all year.

The name "marinara" means "mariner's sauce." There is some debate as to whether the sauce got its start with Spanish or Neapolitan sailors' wives. Since Spain owned Naples during the key years (the first recorded recipe book containing the sauce, written in Naples, is dated 1692), it is a meaningless debate. The important thing is that early on, the healing aspects of tomatoes were discovered, and sailors used the sauce to cure and prevent scurvy.

Tomatoes originated in the New World, and while they probably came from Peru, they were grown at least as far north as Mexico by the time the Spanish sailed. Since the fruit could be dried and was acidic enough to stay preserved, it could be carried long distances. The mariners who carried it could survive at sea without fresh vegetables.

But at some point in history, humankind seemed to stop noticing the connection between the benefits of what we eat and our health. We moved away from herbal remedies toward pills and gadgets. A stiff neck was no longer treated with a warm hand towel wrapped firmly around our neck and fastened with a baby diaper pin. Muscle relaxants became the cure of first resort. I've had friends suffer a torn meniscus and have knee surgery, but most of these injuries used to heal with time and quadriceps exercises.

I admit to admiration for Luddites, but I am not one. I enjoy modern comforts. Still, I cannot help but wonder if we are getting less when we modernize. The stories in the press back me up. It turns out that women of a certain age who take calcium tablets don't benefit as much as women who rely on diet to meet that need. Milk does it better.

I recently read Michael Pollan's *In Defense of Food*, in which he advises us to eat "real" food. I had to laugh when I read that. I remembered my mother scooping something called "Cool Whip" onto some heated pears for dessert. My father leapt to his feet. "What are you doing? Are you feeding our children plastic?" It wasn't plastic, but it also wasn't exactly whipped cream. In 2007, Patrick Di Justo wrote in a *Wired* magazine article entitled "Cool Whip" that it is mostly water and air, although it costs twice as much as homemade whipped cream.

Old-fashioned food is cheaper and better for you. Eating a garlic clove when you start to feel sick isn't nearly as expensive as cold pills; gargling with warm salt water actually feels pretty good (I admit, eating garlic does not) and does relieve most sore throats… but where's the profit?

How many ancient wisdoms have we let fall by the wayside because they were more trouble and less entertaining than being a patient and getting a pill? My mom boiled water to clear her sinuses. I don't know; maybe pills do a better job, but they cost a lot and might do some damage, too.

My father took my temperature by touching his forehead to mine. If mine felt hot to him, I had a temperature. Then came the mercury thermometer. Probably the worst part of that was uncovered in 2001 when 7.4 tons of mercury-contaminated glass from a thermometer factory was found to be polluting the area watershed after having been dumped unprotected. Unilever eventually paid a fine, closed the factory, and cleaned up the mess. At least thermometers aren't made of mercury anymore. Mercury thermometers have been banned in most of the world.

When I was upset, I was given hot milk. When it was hot out, I sat with my feet in a bucket of ice water. Sleeping pills were not even considered. Oh, and generating electricity to cool homes and retail spaces ultimately means that power companies, which typically burn fossil fuels, burn more. This produces greenhouse gases, higher global temperatures, and more air-conditioning.

One of the concerns I have with the miracles of capitalism is that it has overrun the miracles of nature. Corporate profits lie behind much of the erosion of land and the poisoning of air and water. Responsible investors use a battery of approaches to shine light on these issues. But let us also be mindful of what we can do to keep alive the wisdom of prior generations and not fall prey to the marketing myths of ever newer and "better" products.

Of laughter and land mines

*L*ast year I visited a clinic for land mine victims in Phnom Penh, Cambodia, run by an extraordinary organization called Veterans International Cambodia. There you find extreme examples of hope and despair crowded into a small space. The clinic creates individually tailored prostheses known for their flexibility and lifelike qualities. A blind and legless man, a victim himself, assembles customized wheelchairs for children and adults. Physical training helps victims transition to living with disabilities.

While I was there, I met a young girl, perhaps six years old, who was learning to hold herself erect. She was strapped to a large board to train her spine to sense what "erect" feels like—a measure made necessary by years without treatment. To occupy her time and keep her working, a volunteer stood three or four feet in front of her and threw a beach ball her way. As the two played catch, they chatted and giggled. Suddenly the girl let out a peal of laughter so startling that everyone looked up and smiled.

Here I was, seemingly a million miles away from anything I knew. A six-year-old girl is laughing while Cambodia is riddled with land mines. Forty percent of villages have a land mine problem. An estimated six million land mines remain hidden in Cambodia's earth. In her position, I couldn't have laughed.

Yet land mines are still made for profit. We have just celebrated the 10th anniversary of the Ottawa Convention banning them. Most regrettably, the U.S. hasn't signed the treaty. But certain investors, like the Norwegian national pension fund, refuse to profit from companies that make them. It takes homework; many investors unknowingly own shares in land mine manufacturers.

Sadly, the child I saw was a typical victim. Land mine fields are often marked. But a child who can't read doesn't understand the danger—although she's heavy enough to trip the bomb. According to the UN, it could take 100 years to remove Cambodia's mines—and 1,100 years to eliminate land mines worldwide.

As social investors, our emotional response to such an extreme imbalance between profit and harm compels us to take practical action. We invest to contribute to the common good—a clean planet, and a world of peace and justice. And when we imagine that future, joy and laughter are at its core.

———∿∿∿∿∿∿∿———

The courage and hope of the small girl I met in Cambodia were enough to allow her to laugh. But our world should never have allowed her injury to happen. In the West, many of us enjoy a world that's safe and clean; we enjoy good food; we work at jobs that are interesting and beneficial to others; we see the potential for continued prosperity. Universal human dignity would give that girl the same outlook.

———∿∿∿∿∿∿∿———

We must build our shared prosperity together, and define profit—including those we derive from our investments—in terms of mutual benefit. Social investing provides one important way to reach that world. And that's no laughing matter.

Teach your
children well

S ometimes I hear a casual comment, and it nearly consumes me. This happened recently, costing me a full day of research. I was sitting on a yoga mat waiting for a "gentle" class to start, when the conversation taking place next to me drifted into my thoughts.

One woman was talking about having been a stay-at-home mom for several years and how slow the process was getting back into meaningful work. She had my full sympathy as she discussed the passion she had for nutrition, particularly for schoolchildren. I almost joined the conversation but was glad I hadn't when she announced, "I mostly work with private schools. Well, really, those kids are the ones that will graduate and make a success of life and be able to give back."

I was rocked back on my heels. I've read an awful lot about the problems our schools face, but as the daughter of one public school teacher and the stepmother of another, I felt her statement to be horribly blind. I was upset by the idea that the millions who attend public schools had no hope, but I didn't have all the facts to know if she was really wrong.

Does public education hurt or help success? And what did success mean to my fellow yoga student? I guess she probably meant material success. And so my research began. I started with the 10 largest publicly traded companies in America. Despite hours of phone calls, I was unable to find all the data I wanted, but I did find that only one CEO of these 10 large companies definitely went to a private high school. Five definitely attended public high schools. Specifically, I learned that Apple's CEO, Tim Cook, son of a shipyard worker, graduated from Robertsdale High School in Alabama. Exxon Mobil's CEO, Rex Tillerson, graduated from Huntsville High School in Texas. And Jeffrey Immelt, CEO of General Electric, graduated from Finneytown High School in Ohio.

By this point, I was filled with righteous indignation. I decided to look into U.S. Senators on the theory that maybe being able to give back meant political rather than corporate power. The chairs of the standing committees are the most powerful. The Appropriations Committee is probably the single most important, since it decides how federal funds will be spent. Daniel Inouye, its chairman, is a graduate of President William McKinley High School in Hawaii. Ah, you say, but what about the ranking Republican, Thad Cochran? He graduated valedictorian from Byram High School near Jackson, Mississippi.

And while I was on it, *Forbes* magazine's richest 400 were worth a look. It seems that of the top 20, the very richest are about half self-made and half born that way. Self-made billionaire Warren Buffett, casino mogul Sheldon Adelson, and Oracle founder Larry Ellison graduated from public high schools. The richest of all, Bill Gates, did attend a private school. Well, suffice it to say that our public schools have served the nation well, if graduates who become financial or political successes is your guide. Now this isn't meant to be a slam on private schools, nor is it praise for public ones. It is meant to say, don't judge too quickly.

In considering my reaction, I realized that my annoyance with my yoga neighbor's comment was tied to a feeling that it was terribly unfair. I will grant you that our nation's founders created educational institutions largely out of a belief that each individual needed to read the word of God in order to feel His purpose. It wasn't until the 1840s that Horace Mann introduced a system of schools that used grades and offered a uniform education across the towns of Massachusetts. In fact, mandatory education remained little more than a dream until 1918. And look at the 90 years since then. The United States has become a powerhouse of innovation and success. Freed from the historical confines of breeding, the non-elite had the doors opened to them, and in turn sought fortunes and built much.

The victory of universal education is less than 100 years old in this nation. It has succeeded beyond its founders' imaginings. Let's not dismiss the majesty of it. Let's show some pride.

War is hell

On September 21, 2009 all of Italy stopped, came together, and mourned the killing of six Italian soldiers in Afghanistan. As flags flew at half-staff and public offices observed a minute of silence, thousands gathered to honor the fallen. The funeral closed with a display by the Italian air force precision flying team flying in unison over Rome, trailing the red, white, and green smoke of the Italian flag.

Italy's Premier, Silvio Berlusconi, comforted the families of the deceased as the caskets were carried into Basilica of St. Paul's Outside the Walls. "We sent them over there, and they came back dead," said Umberto Bossi, a Cabinet minister and close Berlusconi ally who was at the funeral. Bossi is pressing the government for a pullout of the war.

As an American, I was struck by the difference between the Italian government's response to the loss of soldiers' lives and our own. We went for years without even allowing a photograph of the coffins. I was also struck by the response of the Italian public. Thousands turned out in St. Peter's Square to pray for and honor the dead. Every national television station and CNN International aired the funeral. I tell this story to illustrate that while we in America largely forget that there is a war going on, it is devastating to populations globally.

In the field of socially responsible investing (SRI), the decisions we make about portfolio companies that may benefit from war is an area in which our funds are most different in approach. In America, the first currently existing mutual fund to apply social standards, Pax World Fund, was started by a couple of Methodist ministers who simply wanted to avoid investing their own funds into armament manufacturers. Each new SRI fund since has taken some stand on weapons production, but they are inconsistent one fund from another.

At the base of refusing to benefit from armaments is the question of why. There are those who believe in such a thing as a just war, but do not believe that it is right to manufacture weapons of mass destruction, such as nuclear warheads. There are others who feel war is always wrong, and go farther to say that instruments of killing, such as handguns, are always wrong. Finally, there are those who feel that national defense is important, but that weapons should be manufactured by the government for the government, and not subject to the capitalist push to sell more and more.

Defining what products benefit from war is difficult. Do we penalize the cereal manufacturer who sells to the troops? Do we care that night vision goggles allow accurate killing as well as accurate rescues? In spite of the challenges, each fund sets a standard and follows it. For me, that is what matters. Nowhere else in investing does the question of the morality of war as a capitalist opportunity come under consideration.

One of the earliest truly social shareholder resolutions was filed in 1969. That year *Time* ran an infamous picture on its cover. It showed a young girl running naked as the napalm burned. Socially concerned investors rose to question the morality of Dow Chemical's production of napalm. Since then, we, along with other socially responsible investment firms, have worked on behalf of our shareholders to promote peace. We have helped oppose genocide in Darfur, uncovered corporate links to the military regime in Burma, and shed light on the use of slave labor in Brazil.

It is a sacrilege to send innocents off to face danger and death for anything less than urgent necessity. Yet this war continues, and wars continue globally. I will not cheapen the human cost by recounting the budgetary costs, but I do feel proud to be part of an industry that has always remembered that weapons manufacture and distribution make possible the hell we call war.

The power of the people

Some changes happen very quickly. Occasionally something that has been accepted for generations disappears very quickly. I'm too young to remember the women's struggle to vote, but as I look back at the history of the vote, it seems that once it really began, it happened right away.

I'm not too young to remember the birth of feminism. I grew up believing that I'd probably be a mom, but I might teach kindergarten. There weren't really any sports for me to play, although I did get into a synchronized swimming program in high school.

When I graduated from college, I no longer wanted to teach kindergarten and I wasn't married so I went to typing school. But the change came in a big hurry. Five years later, I was supporting myself as a financial advisor, teaching investment courses, and writing about ethical investing.

I'm not too young to remember the end of smoking. When I was pregnant with my son, who's now 30, the small office I shared with four others was always full of smoke. In fact, after lunch, it was full of cigar smoke. It never even occurred to me that I might ask my fellow workers to show some consideration to a pregnant and uncomfortable woman. But once the ball got rolling, smoking was banned in setting after setting.

The process of long-term sustained change seems to involve a few vital components. First, one needs a countervailing thesis. Women are as much citizens as men are. Smoking is unpleasant and harmful to non-smokers. Next, you need some people to get really, really worked up about it. This vanguard has to be brave about confronting people who disagree with them. After that, the notion is aided by righteousness. Only a fool would consider his wife, mother, daughter, or sister incapable of thought. Only a selfish jerk would poison his or her family and friends while poisoning one's own body. Then comes the toboggan slide, when laws, social norms, and manners all come together to assist, rushing to embrace the new understanding.

Recently, I got a wedding invitation in the mail. Tommy and Brian were getting married. Because Tommy and Brian live in Massachusetts, this same-sex couple was granted access to the institution of marriage, but in most of the U.S. they would not have had the option. Still, it feels a lot like the "smoking is harmful" days. Polls tell us that Americans in every age group don't care about sexual orientation and that all but the oldest Americans believe that granting the right to marry to all is long overdue. In fact, I recently heard openly gay former U.S. Representative Barney Frank describe the right to marry as enjoying a tsunami of support, not just on the Eastern seaboard, not just across America, but increasingly, across Europe.

It feels like such a short time ago that I myself did not see any reason to support homosexual marriage. My friend and colleague in the field of responsible investing, Julie Goodridge, sued for the right to marry. I thought it was an awful lot of work and loss of privacy, and there wasn't anything wrong with living together. But she had been denied the presence of her spouse in the delivery room, and that seemed wrong. She was also denied the benefit of marriage when it came to filing her tax returns, obtaining health care, retirement planning, and estate planning. Nobody really cared that she and Hilary were partners, but everyone wanted to deny them the most natural results. So, I came around. They won that case. And now Tommy and Brian are married.

These things fill me with great hope. I know in my core that important and positive change can occur. What will be next? Will we use the power of common sense to get our proliferating automatic weapons out of the hands of killers? Will we use it to get help, rather than prison sentences, for the addicted? Will we seek systemic means of providing the highest quality education, food, shelter, and healthcare to our population? There is such a thing as the power of the people, and when you see it used, it is thrilling.

$\mathcal{F}$airness will prevail

Early this summer, just after two granddaughters were born into my family—both healthy, and born to loving parents—a colleague came to the door. She was weeping tears of joy. "Do you know what this means?" she said. "Do you know what this means for my son?" She was speaking of the U.S. Supreme Court decision to uphold the right to marry regardless of sexual orientation. After my colleague had given birth two years ago, her wife had had to adopt their son, even though they were married. "That was just demeaning and degrading and wrong," my colleague told me, "but I won't have to adopt our next when my wife gives birth."

Gee, that sort of brings it home. My two granddaughters were born with a host of benefits and assumptions that relied on a mainstream cultural understanding of what the meaning of marriage was. Until today, that understanding refused to allow other newborns—innocents—those same benefits. And while I read that there are many who feel angry and even fear God's revenge over the Court's decision, it is hard to believe that we haven't always understood that the law of the land should stand for every couple who choose to stand before the community and declare themselves married, not simply the majority.

We know that it was a wrong that took a great deal of work to right. And yet in some ways, it took place in the blink of an eye. That gives me great hope. During my life, smoking went from pretty much universally accepted to almost nowhere to be seen. Now same-sex couples have gone from almost nowhere to be seen to pretty much universally accepted. Those are two good changes, and the fact that they came about tells me that society can change.

It is worth remembering what it took to bring about these changes so that we can use the lessons learned to do more. And when I look at these two examples, I see the legal system in the center of it. In the case of tobacco, we had science squelched until the courts forced it into the light. In the case of marriage equality, we allowed pseudo-science, often posing as religion, to squelch logic until court after court forced logic to prevail.

The rule of law is one of the principal means of maintaining democracy. As we look across the globe at those nations that are in shambles, so often it is due to the fact that their leadership became greedy and corrupt and had no laws that applied to them. As an American, I'm fortunate that the continuous assault on the right to trial by jury has not yet succeeded, and that the continuous disdain for trial lawyers has not yet left us without tools to fight for what is right. I know that I will be voting for leaders who will appoint judges who protect "we the people" and give them access to justice.

Justice has sometimes got a harsh sound to it. We think of criminal justice or "an eye for an eye," but there is another sort of justice. It is fairness. What rights a child is born with ought not to differ from the rights another child is born with.

I have cousins in Italy. They are very traditional. When one learned of the birth of my two granddaughters, he sent me these words from Psalm 127:

"Children are a heritage of the Lord."

Otherness

As a nation of immigrants, we sure spend a lot of time worrying about whether immigrants make good Americans. As the daughter of an immigrant, I find myself personally quite fascinated by the discussion. My father didn't come to America for opportunity; he came because he had married an American. He also came because he had a vision of "the land of freedom" and wanted to be a part of it. America had just liberated his country from the Fascists, something he had fought for his entire young life, since he had the misfortune of being the son of a prominent Socialist.

My parents met in an odd sort of way. After World War II, the American government sent thousands of volunteers to rebuild Europe. My mother was one. There she met Italian volunteers who were trying to save street orphans by attempting to locate relatives who might take them in.

One of the Italian volunteers spoke English, and eventually my mother brought him to America as her husband. Italians and Italian Americans were not much liked at the time. There were nasty words used to describe us, and my father could not seem to get a job except from his own kinsmen. He tried importing pasta from Italy, but although it was cheaper than American pasta, Americans found it too chewy for their taste. Yet during my own lifetime, I have seen the visceral disgust that so many New Englanders felt toward Italian Americans completely fall away. And I have seen them come to love Italian-made pasta.

What elements cause the distrust of an ethnic group to emerge and then fade? Can it still happen? The current group that is most central to the debate is the Hispanic population. They represent the big new constituency. Are Hispanics too overwhelmingly different to fit in America? They come for freedom. Freedom from random tyranny and poverty will allow them to prosper and raise families. We understand that, but we also want them to be like us.

The Immigration Restriction League was founded in 1894 by people who opposed the influx of "undesirable immigrants" who were coming from Southern and Eastern Europe. My mother's grandfather, a very fine man in most ways, was one of them. He felt that the new types of immigrants were threatening the American way of life and especially the high wage scale that we Americans enjoyed. He wrote articles about it and was published widely.

His last point, wages, is a tough one. Arguably, if we completely ran out of workers, it seems that we'd be forced, as a nation, to do a better job of bringing those who are currently shut out into the mainstream. I'm not so sure. It is true that during the last few years of President Clinton's administration, unemployment was so low (4.1 percent in 1999) that the papers ran stories of new jobs for the mentally disabled or recently incarcerated. But if you look at the segregated figures, each worker demographic group (Hispanic, Black, elderly, teen) improved, but the harder-hit remained the harder-hit. We did not see the gap between college-educated males and teenagers narrow, for instance. So, worker scarcity does not seem to lead to a fairer distribution of jobs. Meanwhile, most studies indicate that the new immigrant taxpayers support our social security systems, and their purchases help fuel our economic growth.

Nothing is new in the debate over immigration. We still fear otherness, we still fear an unfamiliar new language, and we still fear job or wage loss. This time is not different. The reasons for opposing a path to citizenship have not changed. The actual movement from alien cluster to mainstream citizen has not changed. The acceptance—even celebration—of the ethnicity of our own family's past continues to be appreciated, not abhorred, by our neighbors, but only after a generation or two.

In the end, for me it comes down to the gut. My father was a good man. In spite of a certain amount of prejudice, he made a living, became admired by friends and neighbors, built a modest business cooking eggplants, and left a mark on the world. His simple factory created jobs and taxpayers; his values were key to shaping mine. His life would have been good, very good, if he had stayed in Italy, but America was a shining beacon of something more than a good life: freedom. That is what he craved, and what he found. Should we now deny this to others? I think not.

$\mathcal{B}$lown away

Recently, I found it necessary to be part of what is euphemistically called "an intervention": Intervening in someone's life to try to stop self-destructive behavior and get the person on the road to recovery. Sadly, the person involved, someone who is dear to me, drank for two straight days before I figured out that we had a problem. It is remarkable how easy it is for a determined addict to cover their tracks.

But this is not a tale of gloom. My friend is in a program at present. That program will help to allow sobriety to return. It may also assist in building a resolve to conquer the demons that clearly have dominated of late. After that comes a lifetime of work, and that's what I have been studying. That's where the hope comes in.

From what I can find, a key aspect to recovery is acknowledging that there is logic to the universe that is beyond the individual. This logic is often called God, and a lot of recovery programs speak of giving yourself over to God. It is also called science, harmony, your higher power, and a good many other things. Apparently, when the addict acknowledges this larger logic, he or she is able to more easily defeat the smaller demon.

This reminded me of a concept I'd recently heard about. Rabbi Arthur Wascow is a man whose religion has led him to a lifetime of fighting for the disempowered. He spoke of YHWH, or Yahweh. The original Hebrew word is never to be pronounced. This is made clear by giving it no vowels, rendering the letters unpronounceable. But it is also a core teaching that the word is too sacred to speak aloud. The rabbi had his audience attempt to sound those letters, YHWH. What came out sounded like blowing.

It is a beautiful concept, that the deity is expressed as breath, which is essential to life. Taking it further, all animals breathe. Actually, plants breathe as well. And then the winds that form as the planet turns sustain the life below. Even the more distant sun and other stars fit into this magical breath. As Rabbi Wascow spoke, I could easily see a single, breathing universality.

Sometimes, in a yoga class, I've spent time making that YHWH sound, pacing my own motion, even my heartbeat to it. I had never previously thought of it as universal. That is probably because it is also centering. It helps the yoga practitioner to deepen their pose as it exercises the lungs. Do all the ancient wisdoms hold the sound of breath as a central concept?

I thought of all this as I thought of my dear one. My first action after the act of getting help had been to put my lips together and blow. Now that I've done some reading and some thinking, I wonder if I had known I was uttering a prayer of sorts.

The past few days, I've learned a lot about how to help when the treatment ends. It is important that many of us lend support. We will organize ourselves to take on tasks, perhaps reading groups, perhaps drawing classes, perhaps sailing. We will find means of being present. We know that an addict cannot solve addiction but can live with it and without the alcohol. We will help make that new life fun. In doing so it will make my life more fun. It will enrich me.

I know that a lot of people, probably most people, have trouble with the concept of a "personal" God, or some deity that deals with you one to one. That's a part of recovery that doesn't seem easy to swallow. But the concept of a universal breath seems very easy to give one's self to. Wikipedia says that YHWH is probably related to a prayer that means "that which creates" (I took out gender).

If addiction recovery has to do with strong community and the embracing of that which creates, then it seems achievable. If it is achievable, then I can breathe. I find myself pursing my lips, blowing softly, feeling the relief and hope. I'm sad for my friend and the relations involved but passing through this has caused me to do a good deal of thinking. I think it was time.

People sometimes ask why I don't invest in liquor company stocks. I don't know, maybe I'm being a bit puritanical. But the pervasiveness of alcohol in our society comes at a high human cost. And when you add social pressure, slick advertising, and relentless cheerfulness, drinking can lead to addiction and misery. Myself, I'd rather take a deep breath.

"Myself, I'd rather take a deep breath."

Play your best card

When I was 12, my family moved to Naples, Italy, the city of my father. He had lived in America for 11 years, and he had American children who could not speak Italian at all well. We thought we might stay forever if we liked it and if he could do well there. We only stayed for a year, but during that year I learned many lessons. I don't think I would have learned them as easily if I had never spent time in an ancient and still-troubled city. These are lessons I use most every day.

1. Even card games can be manly displays. Many times, relatives would gather in my grandparents' apartment. After a good meal, the men would take out a special deck containing only 40 cards. The suits were different from ours: gold coins, a bludgeon or club, a sword, and cups. The game, *Scopa*, was played voraciously for hours. The men would taunt each other by displaying captured cards and commenting endlessly over the beauty of, say, the six of clubs. They laughed a lot, and so did I. The seven of gold was the best card and was called *Settebello*. The men would blow kisses to the *Settebello*.

2. There are many languages. As I really learned to speak Italian, I also learned that the Neapolitan language is more than a dialect. It contains ancient Greek words and colorful innuendos that do not exist in "real" Italian. "*Sfizio*" is such a word. It is sort of like going on a lark, having fun doing something silly or without purpose. Extra words are a good thing; they get you thinking about life in a new way.

3. You can trust people sometimes. My grandparents lived in a fourth-floor walk up. And my grandmother was very short, so the steps were a challenge, especially

with groceries. Outside her window, a pulley was rigged. From it hung a basket she could lower to the street. She would lean out the window, shout at a passing boy, and lower the basket with a list and some money. When he returned, she'd lower the basket to recover the groceries and change. Then she'd lower it again with the boy's tip. The boy was always trustworthy.

4. Drunks are not men. There was a man in the neighborhood who would get drunk and stumble down the sidewalk. Everyone despised him. My mom told me it was because when men get drunk, they give up their manhood, and to Neapolitans, manhood is very important.

5. There are some ugly things that happen before food gets to the table. I liked to go to the docks, but that was where the little octopi were brought in in baskets. Men would sit on overturned pails and pluck these creatures out. The men would stick their thumbs into the head, turn the creatures inside out, and cut out the ink sac for one bowl and the body for another.

6. School uniforms are okay. In 1961, when I was there, all children still wore uniforms. Until they were about eight, boys and girls both wore a sort of a blue dress with a white bow in front. I think the boys wore shorts under them. The uniforms were a loud announcement: These are children, not little adults.

7. Old people know things. My grandfather, and most old men of that time in Naples, always had songbirds. He gave me a pair, and I kept them in my room at home. One day, the female bird died. My grandfather came by and told me now the male would die, too, because his heart was broken. In a few hours, the male squeezed through the bars. Why had he never done that before? He flew around the room, and then he fell, dead. Before that, I thought my grandfather was very smart, but this told me he was mystical, too.

I think of my year in Naples a lot. It is part of me and part of why I want to leave the world a bit better than it would have been without me. In the card game *Scopa*, capturing the seven of gold, *Settebello*, is one of the most important ways to win the game. It is worth the most points. There is an expression, "Play your seven of gold"; it means "do your best." That world seems so long ago and so sweet and gentle. I'm glad I lived it. I'm playing the *Settebello*; I'll do my best. It is the least each of us can do.

Innocence

I well remember the last time I fired a gun. I was 12 and crossing the Atlantic on an ocean liner. Skeet shooting was set up off the side of the ship, and my brothers and I were pretty good shots, having had practice in the fields around my grandfather's house in Connecticut. It was fun, but I never really followed it.

My grandfather had trained me to take shots at groundhogs. He hated them and accused them of ruining his meadows. But I was a bit queasy about killing animals, especially dumb ones that just stood there looking into the distance. My own taste ran toward sneaking up on animals and watching them. I was pretty much left to my own devices during hot summer days, and if I went to the spring in the woods, I almost always saw something of interest. If I went a bit farther, I could find a beaver dam. My grandfather wanted to shoot beavers too, so I never told him if I saw one.

Childhood is supposed to be like that. Mine was full of those gentle afternoons. I'd ride a bike to the center of town to watch a movie or bowl at the town hall. In the winter, I'd test the ice on Hawley Pond, and if it held, I'd practice going faster and faster or even backwards. I've been thinking a lot about my sweet innocent self during those years of growing up in Newtown, Connecticut.

The elementary school was brand new when I arrived there for second grade. All of us in my grade put on a show for the rest of the school. It was a pageant of patriotic songs. We dressed up in red, white, and blue; we waved flags and strutted about in unison. Our grand finale was "My Country 'Tis of Thee," and there wasn't a dry eye in the house. Pretty much the whole town showed up at the Sandy Hook Elementary School for that.

When I think of Columbine or Virginia Tech or Aurora, I think only of the massacres. I don't think I understood that they were real places, with sweet meanings for generations of people. It doesn't seem possible that Newtown could have joined the list. What would that have been like? To be seven, to see the man with the gun, to watch as he shot my teacher, my friends, two and three times each before turning to the next, to be six or seven years old and to die at the hands of a monster? It cannot really be that this happened in my Newtown.

President Obama has said that the country must act. I agree. We must no longer ignore public safety and public opinion because some of us have been hoodwinked by corporations into believing that more guns make a safer public. Too much research proves the opposite is true.

As an ethical investor, I don't buy the stocks of companies that make guns. I see it this way. When used as intended, guns kill people. Since monsters can get the guns and turn them on six-year-old children, we need to slow the monsters down.

There seem to be some really easy steps we can take. In 2008, an eight-year-old boy killed himself at a gun club. The boy's father stood behind him and helped his son lift and aim an Uzi. The backfire was more than the boy could handle and the gun kept swinging up and fired into his head. It seems hard to believe that a man handed an eight-year-old an Uzi. It just cannot be up to these dads to know what is safe. There need to be laws.

The massacre in Newtown did something to me. It made me go cold with hatred for the merchants of death. They are no patriots. I know the patriots. The patriots are the rows of seven-year-olds singing, and believing, "Sweet Land of Liberty" in a room that is safe because weapons are not present.

The cycle of life

When I was quite young, our house backed up to the town cemetery. All of us kids thought it was a really good place to play. It was a spot for Capture the Flag and all sorts of running games. We also really liked to play hide-and-seek there, especially at sunset. We'd meet at Kerry.

Kerry was a big family headstone at the back corner. Kerry was one of the first words I learned to spell. On one side of the monument was a meadow, the unused portion of the graveyard, with long grass that sloped towards the woods. On the other side were a great many gravestones, perfect spots to hide behind. Looking back, I find this to be a pleasant thought. The image of children, full of life, frolicking in a place set aside for the remembrance of the deceased, has an uplifting spirit. It never occurred to me to find the place spooky. It was a fun spot. I will admit that I once took flowers off a new grave and brought them to my mother, who promptly told me not to take flowers from graves. I was too young to figure out how she knew they were not from the field, and was quite in awe of her for it.

Suddenly, really in just the blink of an eye, I have not only grown up but also grown old. I write this the day before my birthday. It will be my 66th, which somewhat startles me. I may not be ancient, but I'm old enough to have four granddaughters, and old enough to be thinking of the cycle of life. Birth and death, new life and joy, peace and fear all meld into a sort of seamless stream of consciousness as one ages. Customs change. It isn't so common for children to play in cemeteries these days. This isn't a matter of right and wrong; it is just a difference.

I fear for the future that my granddaughters will face, but I'm nonetheless more at peace with the issue than I was two decades ago. It isn't that humankind is safer; it is more a letting go of anger at things I cannot change. It is finding a gentleness about whatever decline lies ahead. My career, that of advocating for using finance as a means of providing universal human dignity and ecological sustainability, was built on anger. My fury with "the system" for its destruction of beauty and peace just to make a buck fueled the construction of many businesses and, I like to think, was the basis upon which a field—responsible investing—was built.

Now it is time for others to feel the anger, to channel it into a force for good. For me, it is time to reflect and remember, to assist and admire, to enjoy and enable. This is something of a surprise. Had you asked me even ten years ago, I wouldn't have known that I'd actually enjoy aging. One of the best parts is that you get to see how some things turn out.

Professionally, some major impacts have resulted from the work that I had so much to do with. I see that more than 5,000 companies have annual reports on their corporate social responsibility. That never would have happened if responsible investors had not been pushing for information like this for the past 30 years. This is huge. Without our efforts, company management teams never would be spending time calculating costs and benefits for people and the planet.

I read that tens of millions of children who used to work in sweatshops no longer do, thanks to a new, more enlightened corporate attitude when choosing who to do business with. Those children have directly benefited from responsible investors' insistence on tracking how T-shirts and other products get delivered so cheaply to our stores. There is so much to look back upon and say, "In a way, I helped make that happen."

In *The New York Times* I read a story about the failure of companies to adequately assess and inform shareholders about their risks from climate change. The article blamed the Securities and Exchange Commission for inadequately supervising this risk disclosure. There was no mention of me or of my field, but I know that I have written to the SEC, senators, and policy makers many times on this issue, and I know that my peers have kept the pressure on. Now it is going mainstream.

Innocence lost, peace gained, and years passing lead to new views. I know that responsible investing makes a really important difference in the world today, and that the world is better off for it. I have seen the shift.

"Now it is time for others
to feel the anger, to channel it
into a force for good."

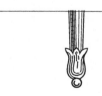

Planet

Simple steps

*A*bout 50 years ago, *The New Yorker* published a cartoon that tickled my father's funny bone, so he got the artist to give him the original. It featured two men looking at a large flip chart on which was drawn a five-story urban type of building, such as you might see in any city. One man was explaining to the other, "It is designed to use modern energy-efficient technology, with windows that open to let cool breezes in." Because of that cartoon, I know that people have been talking about the lost art of energy savings for 50 years or more.

When you start looking at the many ways to preserve energy that the typical Victorian knew but that we have forgotten, it gets a bit disheartening.

My neighbor used to have those outdoor awnings covering each of her windows. When you walked into her house on a hot summer's day, the temperature dropped fifteen degrees. That's because the glass in the window magnifies heat from the sun. If you don't let the sun hit the window, you get a much cooler house. Then she'd open the windows at night to let the cooler air in, closing them again the next morning.

I'll admit, I just don't like air-conditioning. Somehow it just feels wrong. So, I began this article with cooling ideas, but there are other energy savers that have fallen from use. Refrigerators keep getting bigger and bigger, and really, they use energy that our forebears didn't have so didn't waste.

A friend of mine grew up in a house built in 1699, with a cellar, not a finished basement; it had a dirt floor. The family had one room down there with floor-to-ceiling shelves. They stored fresh eggs down there for a month or more. Potatoes, carrots, beets, winter squashes, along with apples and pears and grapes, sat in baskets on the shelves. Jars of jam could be left happily for several years with wax poured over the top. The melted wax adhered to the top of the jelly. Since nothing could get in, not even air, there was no mold, so no germs. Even with the door closed, it got enough heat from the kitchen so that nothing froze, but much could be stored there that today would have to be refrigerated.

I'm not trying to make a case that the world should return to dirt floors in the basement. We are creatures of the generation we grew up in. But it is important to remember that we're not taking the simple steps we could be taking to do our own part in the fight to save the planet from extinction. Climate change is too big a price to pay for personal convenience. So let's get serious about the steps we can take.

First, let's change our lightbulbs. Electric lighting accounts for roughly 25 percent of the energy the average home uses. Yes, the newer, more efficient bulbs cost more up front, but estimates say they save you $20 over the lifetime of the bulb. I don't argue that lower cost is a reason to swap; I only use it to point out how much extra energy the old bulbs are wasting.

Next, let's think efficiency when we consider the purchase of a car. My city has cars you can rent by the hour, and I've found that these work fine for most every need I have. But I do live in a city. If you need a vehicle, at least check the fuel efficiency and factor that into your calculation of the real price of the car. The new electric cars get the miles-per-gallon equivalent of roughly 60 to 120. In other words, they cost you less to fuel (a lot less), and they don't pollute as you drive.

My last thought will surprise some. Let's buy more secondhand. As a society, we create an awful lot of new stuff, and making new stuff uses energy. So does shipping new stuff, packaging new stuff, and lighting the stores that sell new stuff. Buying secondhand is fun and an adventure. It supports local owners and nonprofits. But importantly, it saves energy.

That cartoon on the wall is 50 years old and is as amusing today as it was when it was drawn. We giggle at the thought of claiming that opening windows is the height of new technology. But there is an important message there.

Sometimes simple steps are important.

$\mathcal{A}$ planet is a terrible thing to waste

A recent conversation with a friend got me thinking. This friend had just returned from a conference on species survival and habitat preservation. While there, he learned, to his great surprise, that among a small subset of scientists, he was considered a superstar: the discoverer of a "trigger species." Trigger species are gravely endangered, and their survival requires ecological solutions.

As an undergraduate at Berkeley, my friend had studied amphibians, such as frogs and salamanders. His life eventually led him to a different profession, but he'd maintained some interest in his first love, the ecological implications of species survival. It turns out that an entire global initiative had arisen from his early discovery, and he's considered the father of it. Needless to say, my friend was quite astonished, and so was I.

It got me thinking about the many actions a person undertakes and their potential impact, which can sometimes be world-defining. But it also got me thinking about ecologies. The study of the rainforest or the deciduous forests allows us to achieve balance and protect those areas, but what about the planet itself? Isn't the planet an ecosystem too? And what can I do about it?

Cape Cod in Massachusetts is busy during the summer months, but it's easy to be alone on the shore if you want to be. One day, my son and his friends went out walking and came across a rocky section that wasn't easy to traverse. It was covered with trash, mostly plastic items. They decided to collect it. Several bags later came the conundrum. What do you do with bags of trash when you're staying in a delicate environment where there's no place to dump it? Unfortunately, the answer is: Please, don't create trash.

Are we another precious species, dependent on a unique ecosystem? Are we unwittingly destroying our own ecosystem? I am reminded of Julia Butterfly Hill's question, "Where is away?" Hill is best known for living in a 1,500-year-old California redwood tree for two years in an effort to prevent it from being cut down for the Pacific Lumber Company. Living among the branches, through the seasons, she became remarkably at one with not only the tree but the universe. One night as she stared at the stars, the phrase "throw it away" popped into her mind. It seemed such an awful sentiment. Where is "away"? The world is an island, but a part of a universe. There is no "away."

Here's what my friend and business partner, Steve Lydenberg, does. He sees how many days he can go without throwing away plastic. Even with cities recycling many types of plastic, it's a difficult challenge. For instance, he can't purchase any food to go, except from a couple of conscientious shops. He must carry his own shopping bags. He tries to avoid purchasing plastic pens and chooses products that don't have wrappers. He knows the planet is at stake and he can do less damage, so he takes action.

Then there's my mother. She wraps her sandwiches in wax paper as she sets off to volunteer at the library. Any plastic bags she accumulates get used as trash bags. She cuts the front off any pretty card she receives and uses it as a gift card or postcard. She mends clothing that tears, never buys processed food other than pasta, purchases jigsaw puzzles at secondhand shops and gives them back when she has finished with them. She's 84 and a product of both old Yankee values and World War II, when waste was unpatriotic; the nation needed every ounce of production to be dedicated to the war effort.

Yes, responsible investors can and do raise issues of waste with corporations. We've been important in encouraging sound timbering practices and have been proponents of the "reduce, reuse, recycle" adage. My company's stationery is carefully selected and thanks to work we did with our peers, so is the paper at McDonald's and other large companies. Joining together with others to create an outcome is a goal of responsible investing, and it works.

But today, I keep thinking about what one person can do without ever knowing that what she or he did mattered. Responsibility is also personal and should be embraced by each of us. Caring about the planet means being willing to care for the planet. What the world needs is a few more people who show they care.

ℛepaving paradise

It is time to start placing monetary value on "green and pleasant" spaces. They hold inherent value not traditionally calculated by companies' intent solely on making a profit. The result of disregarding this has been the creation of a landscape that diminishes our enjoyment of life.

What has happened since my youth is a shame. People wanted things, and the quest for more things led to more development. Particularly outside cities, wherever you travel in the U.S., once-pleasant views are blocked by sprawl. The country is plagued by the ubiquitous Route 101 (or whatever), with all its fast-food chains and monotone retail stores. Where once you saw rivers, mountains, corn fields, or majestic forests, now you see concrete and tar. This grindingly depressing environment was economically feasible only because the builder never had to consider (or pay for) the value of "green and pleasant" to the rest of us.

Cities have faced the same plight. The two-story building that had a bit of greenery in front and maybe a rococo trim was replaced by a much taller and plainer one with a footprint right out to the sidewalk. Often the developer kept one wall blank so the next lot could be built upon, leaving the rest of us to look at a large gray flat space or perhaps a gigantic advertisement. This is a well-established right under the law, but it is wrong. The developer took from the neighborhood and pocketed the profit.

Some may argue there is no alternative—that losing a pleasant sight is a necessary by-product of "progress." But that isn't true. Walking down the sidewalk in Madrid recently, I saw a new building towering over older smaller ones, with no windows on the side that would one day be another tower. Yet this time, it was different: A massive garden was affixed to the wall. From afar, you saw a wavy pattern, and standing close, you marveled at the variety of vegetation. The value of the view was intact. A green and pleasant land can be vertical.

Back in the suburbs, prettifying the strip mall may seem like too large a challenge. Nonetheless, the economic situation, coupled with the rise of Internet sales, is forcing a change. Many of the roadside malls are bankrupt, creating eyesores that will eventually mandate new usage. But who will come to the rescue? As local governments try to find users who will at least make the sites a bit more appealing, we see these barren spots giving way to farmers' markets. Local and sustainable businesses are gaining the advantage—almost poetic justice.

This is not meant to be a rant against development. I use these stories to illustrate that almost universally, natural treasures are giving way to further capitalism. This can be a once-pristine lake sacrificed to the nearby oil drilling company, or a sustainable fishery sacrificed to global commercial enterprises that find it cheaper to strip the ocean. Agribusiness convinces unhealthily overfed people in America to eat more beef because it is profitable; meanwhile, children in the Southern Hemisphere starve from lack of grain—which has been used to feed beef cattle. These things happen because corporate profits are counted, while the cost is quietly passed along to society.

There is an answer. First, find out what is going on.

Then disclose it. Finally, assign a value to the loss.

It can be done. Today, Japanese companies must report to their government the cost or benefit to Japanese society of their environmental impact. These detailed reports are models of what could be done across the full range of issues. Responsible investors understand that data, like the Japanese reports, can be a valuable tool for social change. We have played and continue to play an important role in shaping capitalism to incorporate people and the planet. By demanding extra financial information, we strive to expose the "costs go to society, profits come to me" rules by which certain big companies play. We believe the solution is to rewrite the rules of finance in a way that accounts for the total costs of corporate behavior, not just those currently required on financial statements.

I'm sure we all feel sad when we remember a once-wonderful spot paved over to put up a parking lot. What we haven't yet realized is that as investors, we have the ability to shape the decisions that can help other places avoid ending up like this.

℘reserve our wonder

I will admit that I've never been particularly careful about honeybees. As a kid, I'd catch them in jars and threaten my younger brother with them. As a gardener, I find it fun to stare hard and watch as they bob in and out of the blooms, covering their legs with yellow pollen. I don't worry about getting stung. It doesn't take much to start noticing the difference between wasps and honeybees. The honeybees are fuzzy. They don't want to sting you.

My garden has become a bit of a haven for bees and for butterflies. I like to watch them, so I always try to have something flowering to tempt them in. But last year, it was July before I had any good bees. That was really late and I was really worried. It has been a number of years since I've seen bats in my yard. They used to come swoop around each summer evening, putting on a show for me. I don't want to lose bees, too.

I've been reading that there is an international phenomenon of colonies of bees just dying. A scientist at Harvard recently wrote a study that implicated the pesticides used on many crops. Of course, the company making the pesticide said the study was full of holes. One line of thinking was that maybe cell phones were the cause. But a few countries in Europe stopped using the pesticide in question a couple of years ago and their bees came back.

That strikes me as a pretty big coincidence, if true. In fact, it's beginning to feel as if we're experimenting on the planet, and that makes me mad.

When do we stop experimenting this way? It's been 50 years since Rachel Carson published *Silent Spring*. Her revelations about the impacts of DDT showed that pesticide was devastating. Fifty years later, we still haven't admitted that sometimes it is a lot better to prove safety before approving products for widespread use. It's a commonsense argument, but there are those who worry more about the economic impact of not using the newfangled product. This makes no sense to me. The line of reasoning pits a known economic benefit against an unknown cost. Should the cost be, as it was with diethylstilbestrol, or DES, that for at least three generations those exposed develop cancers, are born with intersexual characteristics, and now appear to have permanently affected DNA chains? And the benefit there was not to the mothers-to-be. They took it to ease nausea, but it didn't do much about that. The only benefit was corporate profit.

Back to the honeybees. I did some looking around and there is a lot of information about the bee collapse and the economic costs of it. Almond growers, blueberry growers, orange growers ... in fact, any farmer with a crop that flowers needs bees. Trucks with hives drive around the country bringing bees from place to place, charging farmers for the service. The estimates you read are mostly about the $15 billion worth of American crops that depend on the honeybees. Then there are the honey business and other support businesses. That seems like a lot of economic impact, but it is being ignored so far.

The jury is out on this one. In the end, it may be that colony collapse disorder is the result of solar storms or some other oddity. But I'm ready to bet that when we get to the bottom of this, we are going to find out that the cause is rushing ahead with some great new product without regard to the broader implications of using it.

I used to think my mother was funny. Way back when, we went to a new store with a new parking lot. She complained, "Why do they have to make such an ugly parking lot? It wouldn't kill them to put in some trees and shrubbery."

"In a parking lot?" I giggled.

"Just because you need it doesn't mean it has to be awful," she retorted.

Now I think she was prophetic. We may need ways to progress, but we don't need to degrade our environment to do so. We don't need to be awful. Haven't most of us enjoyed a lazy summer day watching the bees dip in and out of flowers? Haven't most of us been treated to hot water, lemon, and honey to cure our ailments? Fifty years after *Silent Spring*, 25 years after the California Condor Program, can we take a moment to assure ourselves that we are preserving the wonders we now enjoy?

*D*iving into the data

A nice bonus comes when you buy a new pair of Timberland shoes. A label on the box marked "Our Footprint" tells what percentage of your shoes was made with renewable energy, how much of them are free of toxic polyvinyl chloride (PVC) or made of "eco-conscious materials," and what portion of the shoebox is recycled (100 percent). The label also reveals how many trees the company is planting.

This kind of point-of-purchase disclosure is becoming increasingly common. Packages in supermarkets bear the nutritional details about the food they contain, and restaurants in some cities must reveal the calories and nutritional content of their food. Shoppers at Whole Foods Market can choose ocean-caught fish over farm-raised.

As a socially responsible investor, I welcome this. What's published gets measured, and what's measured gets evaluated and improved. But even the best "micro" reporting on a product-by-product level can't take the place of macro reporting. (Timberland, I should note, reports well on both the micro and macro levels.)

Carbon emissions are one indication of the need to look at the bigger picture. Emissions per product are useful, but we have to ask about overall emissions, too. Ultimately, this is the only factor that matters for the environment. For instance, Japanese companies are required to report greenhouse gas emissions and set targets for reductions. But those targets aren't enforced, and companies stress emissions reductions per unit rather than overall corporate numbers.

One company, however, has responded to criticism by gradually shifting its emphasis from per-unit to overall emissions: Sony. At the leading entertainment and technology firm, its management believes demonstrating transparency and accountability will strengthen Sony's public image.

Responsible investors like transparency—and not only on the environmental front. Worker fatality data provide one measure of how well a company protects its employees. But some companies avoid disclosing the overall number of deaths by reporting a smaller number for each subsidiary. In Europe, we discovered some cement companies reported no data on fatalities during certain years—an omission that sent up a red flag, causing our analyst there to dig deeper. She didn't like what she found: an increase in deaths. By seeking and requesting consistent data, social investment researchers establish a baseline that makes it possible to assess a company's improvement (or deterioration) over time. It's important work.

Thankfully, some companies are already doing an impressive disclosure job. The French auto parts company Valeo, for instance, reports on a variety of environmental indicators, including consumption of water and energy, generation and re-use of waste, and emission of CO2. Valeo integrates the data into its annual report rather than publishing it separately.

The Global Reporting Initiative (GRI) represents a significant step towards offering consistent data. The GRI provides a framework for consistent reporting so "disclosure on economic, environmental, and social performance [becomes] as commonplace and comparable as financial reporting."

Timberland has broken new ground in disclosing the impact of its operations on people and the planet. We thank them, and hope that someday soon the leadership at every company will do an equally good job of reporting on both the micro and macro levels. Until that day, the detective work that social researchers like ours carry out every day will remain time consuming but essential. The work enables us to compare one company's performance with another's, identify unacceptable behavior, and give civil society the tools to pinpoint issues that need public action. Responsible investors use social research to create an infrastructure of transparency in reporting.

In fact, it's our mission.

Back to nature

For most of my life, I have enjoyed taking long walks by myself in the woods and fields. When I was a young girl, these walks might have lasted a couple of hours. We lived in the Berkshire foothills, so the woods were hilly and full of boulders. As I grew into my teens and twenties, I spent time on Cape Cod and learned about walking over sandy beaches and rocky shores. In recent years, I've largely returned to the woods, where beaten trails are shaded and filled with discoverable wonders.

Walks provide a person with a chance to accomplish a great deal. One gets a bit of exercise, a chance to meditate, a chance to discover and, for some, the thrill of exhaustion. As a young girl, I could walk through woods that led to a cow farm. It was only because of an old stone wall that I knew a farm had once been on that location. There was a spongy spot marking a shallow spring, and it was surrounded by a yellow flower I knew was cowslip because I was a Girl Scout and studied such things.

Once, as I was resting against a fallen tree that often had bugs and mushrooms on it, a small bird stopped nearby. We locked eyes and stared at each other for a long time. When I went home, I tried to identify it but failed. Another area had small birch trees, some white and some black. The black birch has bark that is sweet, like spearmint, and I'd stop and suck on bits of it. The thin white birch trees were supple. I could pull their heads low and grab a spot. Then with a little jump I'd be lifted off my feet and gently set down in another spot.

Pristine natural environments give us a gift, and that gift is a lasting one. Pristine places are important. Much as I love the manicured parks of the great cities, and much as I love the manicured little garden on my own land, it was the earlier experience of untouched places that gave me the ability to find peace in a bird's stare.

Today, I work with ethical investors, and I recognize that our natural environment is an important partner to humankind and to corporations. Corporations depend heavily on a functional natural ecosystem for so many things, but do they recognize that in a partnership there is give and take? That's what ethical investors care about. For example, most U.S. home-building companies have a business model that is not great for the planet. They find a pristine place and put in roads and yards and houses. The houses they build have terrible carbon footprints and must be arrived at by car, another environmental problem. But in England, the laws are different. Houses are frequently built on old brownfields and other land that has been despoiled. These houses are situated near public transit and bike lanes and are ecologically designed to function as a small village. The website of one company speaks of building around the centuries-old hedges that stood on the land.

So, there is good news. Climate change has not gone unnoticed by institutional investors, who for some years now have been putting pressure on corporate leadership to disclose their carbon footprints, to reduce their waste, and to manage their affairs with greater ecological efficiency. There is also good news on the corporate side as more and more companies take steps to do a better job.

Corporations in and of themselves are a problem, but they are not the only one. They survive by selling what people believe they need, or at least want. Who has not seen photographs of children living in favelas built on garbage heaps? Who has not seen photographs of children dipping a cup into a barrel of water, a barrel clearly labeled as containing hazardous materials? These children will never take a long walk out to where the birch trees sway. You and I are the problem, and the reason is our uncontrolled consumption.

Face it: Those reading this column have more than they need. A small home with sparse furnishings and a couple of changes of clothes was plenty for millennia. But because we want more, we feed the beast. And the beast of capitalism finds ways to get us more stuff at a price point we feel good about. That means creating externalities, like not caring where our T-shirt was made or how the copper was mined. We privatize profit to get to get ourselves stuff, while channeling the health and environmental costs onto those poor young children.

It is important that we enjoy and protect pristine spaces. It is also important that we live without every delight our minds can imagine. The pristine space and natural joys of childhood are giving way to our quest for stuff; when you think it through, that's just wrong.

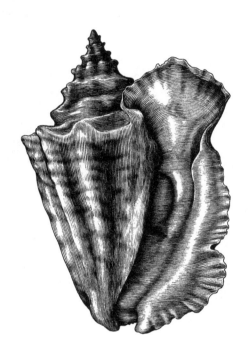

Damned lies and statistics

As a kid on Cape Cod, I'd get really frustrated with a ground-dwelling bird that lived all around us. The Virginia quail (or bobwhite) had the most annoying call. At dawn it would start in, tentatively, "Bob? Bob White?" This would repeat until you thought you'd lose your mind. While I still spend much of my summer on Cape Cod, I haven't heard a bobwhite in 20 years.

During long summer days, I'd crawl around the boulders and pull out handfuls of mussels, bring them home, and feast. I can't find them anymore. Nor do scores of conches roll up after a storm. And I could swear there are far fewer lightning bugs in the evening.

I love the natural world and want to protect it. That's why I felt so angry with myself recently. I was on an airplane and a man next to me told me he was an electrical engineer and noticed I like numbers, too. I said I was playing Sudoku and it didn't require math. But he said no one understands simple math: Vice President Al Gore's formula was wrong and there was no climate change. The storms were no worse than usual. We were all being played for chumps.

I didn't fight back. I hadn't spent the time memorizing a few salient facts. My experiences informed me that everything is changing but I couldn't quantify it. So here's what you need to know if this happens to you. All this comes from the Environmental Protection Agency (EPA) website: epa.gov/climatechange.

Each year the Audubon Society conducts a Christmas bird count, which shows that bird migrations have shifted. Bird species in North America have moved their winter locations north by an average of 35 miles since 1966, with a few species shifting by hundreds of miles. Next: Plant hardiness zones have shifted.

Large portions of the U.S. have seen shifts northward by one zone since 1990. Gardeners rely on these charts to know what will survive in their regions. The EPA site shows the changes. It is startling.

The time between last frost and first frost has long been measured. In the U.S. West, the growing season is 20 days longer now. In the eastern U.S., it's six days longer.

Glaciers worldwide have lost more than 2,000 cubic miles—yes, miles—of water since 1960, which has contributed to the observed rise in sea levels. The average global absolute sea level increased at an average rate of 0.06 inches per year from 1870 to 2008. From 1993 to 2008, average sea levels rose at a rate of 0.11 to 0.13 inches per year—almost double the long-term trend.

And as we are all experiencing, the storms are worse. A larger percentage of precipitation comes in very intense, one-day-only events. Eight of the top 10 years for extreme one-day precipitation have occurred since 1990. (These figures pre-date the tornadoes of 2011.) Furthermore, the heat is worse. The percentage of the U.S. affected by heatwaves has risen since the 1970s, with an alarming rise in very high nighttime temperatures.

Now I know a few facts that prove to me that the climate is changing. They aren't as useful as the charts one sees, but anyone can use them. My airplane buddy probably wouldn't care about the EPA, but it does have documentation about climate change on its website.

My airplane buddy wouldn't care what the Securities Exchange Commission thinks. But it acts like it believes in climate change, releasing guidelines on when to report risks concerning climate change: "Physical Impacts of Climate Change: Companies should also evaluate for disclosure purposes the actual and potential material impacts of environmental matters on their business."

The Investors' Network on Climate Change includes 100 institutional investors, with assets totaling $10 trillion. Investors managing trillions are not generally chumps. And they have formed a coalition to address the challenge of a changing climate. Yep. I guess I'm a believer in climate change. Socially responsible investors have used climate change criteria in stock selection, filed shareholder resolutions to ask for climate change risk reporting, and spurred the growth of green funds. We've tried to be a voice of responsibility to the planet, our only home.

I don't dare hope for a reversal of damage done; I doubt the bobwhite, mussels, and conches will be abundant on Cape Cod. But when strangers on airplanes spout off, it is sobering. I only hope Americans will wake up so we can change our ways in time.

*W*hat is normal?

In the *Huffington Post*, the headline read, "South Carolina Rainfall Is Worst in a Thousand Years, Gov. Haley Says." That was an exaggeration. Most experts said it was the worst rain in "only" 500 years. I was there, which got me to thinking: Was this a sort of déjà vu all over again? Yes, it was October 2011 and I was in Dublin, Ireland, for the most rain ever recorded in that city. And then there was last winter in Boston, when just over 110 inches of snow gave us an all-time record.

It may be tempting to blame the weather on my presence, but that seems unlikely. Inside of five years I had been present at three dramatic weather events. If this is happening to me, it is happening to pretty much everybody. The weather is changing dramatically.

In the discussion on climate change, some scientists are struggling to speak a language that we can feel deeply enough to change our ways. NASA has a compilation of statements online. One of the earliest American scientific voices they cite came from the American Chemical Society in 2004: "Comprehensive scientific assessments of our current and potential future climates clearly indicate that climate change is real, largely attributable to emissions from human activities, and potentially a very serious problem."

That surprised me. I hadn't expected that the American Chemical Society would have voiced such an opinion. It was followed by concurring statements from many others, including the American Geophysical Union, the American Medical Association, and the American Meteorological Society.

On the one hand, this is such a huge issue that I feel a bit helpless, but as I reflect on it, I'm actually doing quite a lot, in my own way. First, as a responsible investor I decide which stocks to buy only after looking at their environmental impacts. To do that, I need data; to get the data, I need to badger companies; and to get my kind of investor off their backs, companies have started publishing sustainability reports. There are now more than 4,000 companies tracking the progress they're making toward lower emissions. That is important, because big companies can greatly speed up or greatly slow the problem.

Next, as a responsible consumer I keep some facts in mind. I don't need avocados every time I shop. I can save my avocado purchases for days when there are organic avocados available. In fact, I can shop organic for baby clothes, sponges, and a whole lot of other things. I can also conserve electricity and fuel; it is pretty easy to turn off lights and to drive less. The more I started counting up ways I could help, the more I realized I was already helping.

Mitigation and adaptation: these are the two prongs of response to climate change. Switching out of fossil fuels into other energy sources, like solar power, slows climate change and mitigates the problem. Building seawalls to try to prevent the shoreline from crumbling does not slow climate change, but it does allow us to adapt to the problem. In academic circles, there seems to be a vast preference for mitigation strategies as well as an acceptance of the immediate need for adaptation strategies.

Unfortunately, the average citizen can't do much more than adapt. It is much simpler to get more water efficient sprinklers than it is to reverse the climate change that has led to less rainfall. Too much good thinking is going into plugging the dyke rather than reducing our dependency on fossil fuels.

Last winter, I adapted to the record-breaking snow by spending a lot of money having snow shoveled off my roof and taken away in pickup trucks. It took four of them. I wonder: Did that many trips by pickup trucks cost the world more than my ice dams would have cost me? This year I mitigated the problem by not driving through the floods. It was a pretty easy decision, since the roads were closed. But I did ride my bicycle between showers, just to see what it looked like out there. When the water got so high that I couldn't pedal, I jumped off. It was up to my thighs. Standing water up to my thighs on a road isn't normal; if it were, I'd have experienced it before. Climate change is real, and it is getting scary. Let's move beyond adaptation to mitigation, and let's start today.

Saving energy and buying time

———— ❖ ————

The Earth's population has grown staggeringly in a single lifetime, from less than 3 billion in 1960 to 6.7 billion today. And with China and India poised to become consumer societies on an enormous scale, it's natural to assume that demand for energy will grow in lockstep with population.

We tend to think that demand for energy is inelastic—that people will insist on burning a certain amount of fuel to maintain their ways of life. The alternative, as energy executives tried to tell us during the energy crisis of the 1970s, is to "freeze in the dark." For those of us who believe reversing global warming is the most urgent challenge of our time, this is a frightening thought.

Yet 30 years ago, it was already obvious that some people were managing to live well on a much more modest energy budget than we in the West do. With new technologies, it's possible to trim our energy use even more—and buy some desperately needed time.

Oil executives don't like the idea that we can get along with less of their product. But a recent article in *Financial Week* argues that we can save more energy than we think. After world oil consumption peaked in 1979, the article says, high prices caused the demand for oil to drop. The world's oil consumption didn't surpass its 1979 level for a decade, and U.S. oil consumption didn't regain its 1979 level until 18 years later, in 1997.

The same thing may be happening again. The number of vehicle miles driven in the U.S., for example, fell in March of this year for the first time since 1979. That number continued to drop in April and May.

The difference between 1979 and 2008 is that we have new techniques and technologies to save energy without depriving ourselves of goods, services, and hours on the road. As social investors, many of us strive to invest in the companies that are bringing these techniques and technologies to the market.

The spiral-shaped bulbs of compact fluorescent lights (CFLs) have become a symbol of these new approaches. According to the advocacy group Environmental Defense (formerly the Environmental Defense Fund), changing just one 75-watt light bulb to a CFL eliminates about 1,300 pounds of global warming pollution.

Technology for wind power has advanced significantly. Vestas Wind Systems of Denmark, the world's leading supplier of wind power, claims a 28 percent market share with 33,500 wind turbines in place. This year, the company said it received an order for 232 turbines from a division of the China Guangdong Nuclear Power Group, which has been diversifying away from nuclear power and its radioactive-waste challenges.

Leaders at other companies are finding innovative ways to manufacture products with less energy. The directors of SSAB Swedish Steel, for example, say 60 percent of the steel the company produces comes from recycled scrap metal, which can be smelted in electric arc furnaces or mini-mills that are more energy-efficient than traditional blast furnaces. The company's blast furnaces require coke as fuel, and the company says it uses the gas from coke furnaces as a source of energy for other operations. Other gases generated in steel production are used to make electricity and heat homes in the area.

* * *

The global climate crisis is urgent and enormous. The future itself is at risk. But meeting the challenge isn't impossible. If as consumers and investors and taxpayers we support new energy technologies, we can help give ourselves the breathing room we need to cope with global warming and transition to a more sustainable way of life. It's not too late.

"It's not too late"

Counting carbon

*T*he planet is in trouble. Whether you call the problem global warming or climate change, we're facing an environmental crisis that's already reshaping life on Earth. Everything from polar bears to insurance companies will be affected. Smart investors—whether they care about the fate of the Earth or not—should take notice and become part of the solution.

As companies create fuel-efficient cars, lower-cost solar cells and energy-saving light bulbs, investors provide the capital needed for research and development and to bring these products to a broader market. In search of profit as well as a better world, venture capitalists help get startup companies off the ground, and concerned investors in publicly traded stocks help push bigger companies to devote more resources to sustainable solutions.

Responsible investors help in a more subtle but perhaps more important way: By demanding the numbers that enable us to know which projects are effective and which aren't, which companies are engaged in greenwashing and which are helping to save the planet—and perhaps themselves. Some companies are well positioned to prosper in a carbon-constrained environment, while others will bear substantial costs to adapt and some will simply go out of business. Without data, investors are unable to distinguish winners from losers reliably.

The urgency of the crisis has spurred a number of creative solutions: some large and complex, some small and specific. What all of them have in common is that they rely for their effectiveness on accurate reporting.

In the U.S., the Obama administration has proposed a cap-and-trade system for regulating carbon emissions. Companies with emissions under the limit can sell emissions "credits" to other companies that would otherwise find it hard to comply. The European Union Emission Trading System has already become the largest such scheme in the world.

Many companies are doing their parts. Kyocera and Sharp, from Japan, have made a major commitment to solar power, and Vestas Wind Systems in Denmark dominates the field of wind power. Philips has spent a large portion of its R&D budget on LEDs and other energy-efficient lighting products. Herman Miller, a U.S. company, uses a cogeneration plant to burn its waste, which provides heat and air conditioning for its central plant along with some of its electricity.

CEOs of some companies are even saying "Regulate me." In May, more than 500 business leaders at the World Business Summit on Climate Change asked governments to make a strong commitment to cutting carbon emissions. Certainty on emissions targets would help them make long-term decisions, they said, and a level playing field would prevent industries located in countries with tough emissions rules from losing out to those where regulations are more lax.

In Japan and the European Union, companies are already required to report carbon emissions. The U.S. is lagging behind, but a new and more environmentally conscious administration may change that. In the meantime, social investment funds have pushed companies for greater transparency in carbon reporting. Because healthy forests play a crucial role in the fight against climate change, my firm has made sustainable forestry a focus of our shareholder activism. We've also encouraged energy companies in our portfolios to report their carbon emissions, and as a member of the Carbon Disclosure Project we've urged companies worldwide to do the same.

When accurate mandatory carbon emissions reporting becomes the norm worldwide, we'll be better positioned to assess what can be done by industries, companies, and governments to reduce emissions, increase operating efficiency, and most important, protect our planet and ourselves.

*W*ater, water, everywhere

As a child, I grew up in a dairy farming community. There weren't many kids around, so I learned to be alone. I enjoyed wandering across the cow field to a very small stream that ran through the farm. I'd spend hours waiting for tadpoles in the water or salamanders in the mud to reveal themselves.

That farm is gone; 50 houses now occupy the space. The stream is gone, as are the many life forms that depended on it. It's happening all over the world. Fresh water is essential to human life, yet it's becoming an increasingly scarce resource. Now the scarcity has moved from hurting tadpoles to hurting people.

As the world's population continues to grow, so do the demands on the supply of water. Many countries, especially in the Southern Hemisphere, face horribly inadequate water supplies. These don't simply lead to discomfort; they lead to misery and death. According to the UN's Food and Agriculture Organization (FAO), 3,800 children die every day from diseases associated with the lack of safe drinking water and proper sanitation. The FAO found that 1.1 billion people don't have access to the necessary five to 13 gallons (20 to 50 liters) of freshwater to meet their basic needs, and 2.6 billion people don't have proper sanitation.

The way a company uses water can help alleviate suffering. In India, PepsiCo faced charges that its bottling plants drastically lowered local water levels and contaminated groundwater. In response the firm decided to work on watershed protection, sanitation, and preservation. One outcome, the use of reverse osmosis filters, conserves 280 million gallons (a billion liters) of water each year. If every company instituted sound water conservation policies, the impact would be enormous.

But there's a role for people, too. We can help, in the twin roles of consumer and investor. As investors, much has happened. One example occurred when responsible investors approached the semiconductor industry about water usage. Cleaning electronic chips requires highly purified water. It can take two gallons (eight liters) of ordinary water to yield a gallon of "ultra-pure water." Intel reports that as of 2008, it had invested more than $100 million in water conservation projects and now reclaims more than 3 billion gallons (12 billion liters) of water a year. When investors advocate, they have impact.

Consumers play an important role, too. At Domini Impact Investments, we've joined with the many individuals and small businesses that have taken the "Think Outside the Bottle Pledge" sponsored by Corporate Accountability International (CAI). We no longer purchase bottled water for the office; we provide filtered water and seltzer machines for employee use. We did this after learning that for each gallon of water that's bottled, three gallons (11 liters) of water are used to make the bottle. CAI tells us that Americans bought 8.8 billion gallons (33 billion liters) of bottled water in 2007; that means 26.4 billion gallons (more than a trillion liters) were consumed making plastic in which to put that water. To make matters worse, people don't recycle plastic water bottles as much as they do soft drink bottles, probably because of differing refund laws. The Container Recycling Institute estimates that in 2005 this "wasting" or non-recycling added almost 2 million tons of PET bottles to the waste stream.

Addressing the problem of water scarcity will take the energy and creativity of governments, non-profit groups, and ordinary citizens. The little stream where I once spent lazy summer afternoons is gone. For me, the child who watched as a snapping turtle dragged itself out of the water to lay eggs, that spot was almost sacred. When I returned to see it 40 years later, I felt as if a dear friend had died. Yes, people want things. But that doesn't excuse irresponsible behavior with our natural resources, resources that are both life-giving and soul-filling.

Ode to the ocean

My relationship with the oceans has been entirely recreational. Ever since I was a child, I've enjoyed searching the shores for special places where snails resided, or unique shells could be found. Small-boat sailing brings challenge and excitement to a warm summer day as one struggles to keep the tide and the wind directions firmly in mind while actually getting somewhere. Occasionally a fish would jump, or I'd even come across a floating sunfish, basking, I suppose, in the sun. But during all my years of play and exploration, I'd never seen what wonders the ocean holds.

I recently had the chance to enter into the magical, mystical world of the creatures that seed life on planet Earth. Imagine entering a room filled with large posters of the most fantastical beings, brought to the surface through the power of enormously powerful magnification. Creatures so small that they are one-tenth the width of a strand of hair, that live as complex a life as any we have seen yet are completely ignored in (at least my) day-to-day life.

Seeing these beings blown up to "human size" reminded me of a conversation about eternity I'd once had. I'd found myself conversing with a rocket scientist on a flight across the country. Since he was a defense contractor, I was trying to keep it light, and I asked him if he thought space was infinite. He surprised me by saying size was infinite—that the atoms that held my body together were as distant from one another as the stars we see at night. That was how he knew there was infinite wisdom, God. I don't know if he was right about the distance of atoms, but it was a powerful image.

Most of us have had a chance to stare at the midnight sky and become lost in the infinity we behold. It stills one. The mind recognizes patterns and hazes; the eye picks up the sudden shift as a shooting star falls. If the distant suns were sentient beings, they would be unable to see us without fabulous microscopes. If they did see us, they would presume that we were too little to think, too unformed to have purpose. As I wandered through the ocean microbes gallery, looking at the complex array of entities before me, I thought of that, and of infinity in size, and infinite wisdom.

These microbial beings form the basis for life, at least in the ocean. Some are a combination of plant and animal, sustaining themselves both with light and by eating. Others synthesize sunlight so efficiently that commercial solar energy projects are studying them for clues. Some sea microbes have land cousins, and this leads to innovative ideas. One has a land cousin that causes malaria. It may be that the ocean version will be a source of vaccine for that scourge, just as exposure to cowpox was used to prevent smallpox.

But this is not a story of overlooked solutions; rather, it is a story of wonder, infinity in a drop of seawater, answers by the thousands, floating about us and waiting to be found. These tiny microbes create half the oxygen on earth—every other breath we take is thanks to tiny ocean creatures. Furthermore, many of them process—a word that roughly translates as "eat"—greenhouse gases. They may be able to slow the devastation to our atmosphere.

My evening at the gallery was a wonderful reintroduction to the majestic and delicate web of life. I hope that we continue to learn of new life forms on Earth and that we continue to be humbled by them. Meanwhile, I'll enjoy the summer waves in an entirely different way.

ℋarmful chemicals
we can do without

When I was a child, my parents gave me a "science kit" that contained samples of rocks, minerals, and metals. It was wonderful. I'd pull out a sample of quartz and memorize what it looked like. Soon I would be able to spot it out in the wilds of New England. But I could never find my three favorites: asbestos, lead, and mercury.

Asbestos was intriguing. You could pull fibers off it and even though they looked like little feathers, they wouldn't burn. Lead looked so small and weighed so much; it seemed impossible. And mercury would roll up into a ball and could be split and the bits would come together again as a new ball. I guess hazardous materials have been in toys for a long time.

Over the past year we have seen repeated recalls of toys and baby bottles and even children's jewelry. During my childhood, companies were still lying about the safety aspects of asbestos, lead, and mercury, but at least these businesses labeled them. Today, the situation is worse. We don't know what is in everyday products. Incredibly, the Environmental Protection Agency (EPA) is only beginning to review chemicals in wide use to determine safety, and the Food and Drug Administration (FDA) doesn't even regulate certain products, like cosmetics, that contain numerous toxic chemicals.

The FDA is turning its attention to bisphenol A (BPA), found in hard, clear polycarbonate bottles and the linings of canned foods, to name just two common uses. While I appreciate the effort, the book *Our Stolen Future* broke the story more than a decade ago that BPA almost certainly mimics hormones in the body, leading to a host of unpleasant effects. Why did the FDA stall for a decade?

Canada has already banned BPA in baby bottles and *The New York Times* columnist Nicholas Kristof wrote that doctors at Mount Sinai School of Medicine in New York City suggested he not microwave food in plastic, not put plastic in the dishwasher, and avoid plastic with recycling numbers 3, 6, and 7.

On the EPA's list are phthalates, used in vinyl and cosmetics; brominated flame retardants, added to electronics and other goods; perfluorinated compounds used in non-stick coatings and food packaging; some paraffins, used in lubricants; and benzidine, used in dyes and pigments. My firm has filed shareholder resolutions asking companies to address the risks of a number of these toxins, as well as parabens, a preservative used in countless products. These chemicals are known to be dangerous to humans.

The problem goes beyond possible harm to you from eating soup from a plastic bowl that released a toxin when you heated it. It has entered the life cycle chain. Our babies are born with dangerous chemicals already at work in their bodies. In a recent report, the Environmental Working Group found that the umbilical cords of 10 newborns contained 287 chemicals; nine out of 10 contained BPA. Of these 287 chemicals, 180 cause cancers in humans or animals, 217 affect our brains and nervous systems and 208 cause birth defects. I'm going to bet these mothers did not knowingly ingest arsenic during pregnancy. The natural environment exposed them to it because our environment itself is polluted.

It doesn't need to be this way. We don't need the harmful chemicals for the products we make. There was a time when all insulation contained asbestos. Although the damage caused by asbestos was known to the ancient Greeks, who used condemned slaves to mine it, our building companies found it to be cheaper than alternatives and so condemned thousands to die. Although mercury poisoning was recognized in Elizabethan times, leading to the term "mad hatter" (mercury was used for making felt from animal pelts), our thermometer manufacturers, who packaged a toxic element in fragile glass, found it to be cheaper than alternatives and so condemned thousands to die.

I am grateful that our government is finally assessing the danger of using these commonplace chemicals, but it doesn't make me feel better. What would make me feel better is a regulatory system; that will only happen when business leaders care as much about human health as they do about profit.

Silent spring, again

S ilence can be a source of healing, a refuge from the stress of modern life, and a pathway to enlightenment. Or it can have a more sinister meaning.

In 1962, Rachel Carson, an accomplished biologist and popular writer, published a book that would change our attitudes toward our planet. *Silent Spring* began on a deceptively peaceful note, in a chapter called "A Fable for Tomorrow." "There was once a town in the heart of America," Carson wrote, "where all life seemed to live in harmony with its surroundings. The town lay in the midst of a checkerboard of prosperous farms. ... In autumn, oak and maple and birch set up a blaze of color that flamed and flickered across a backdrop of pines. Then foxes barked in the hills and deer silently crossed the fields, half hidden in the mists of the fall mornings." But something went wrong in this idyllic town: "There was a strange stillness. The birds, for example—where had they gone? Many people spoke of them, puzzled and disturbed. The feeding stations in the backyards were deserted. The few birds seen anywhere were moribund; they trembled violently and could not fly. It was a spring without voices. On the mornings that had once throbbed with the dawn choruses of robins, catbirds, doves, jays, wrens and scores of other bird voices there was now no sound; only silence lay over the fields and woods and marsh."

Millions of Americans responded to this ominous vision, making *Silent Spring* not only a massive bestseller but one of the most influential books in the country's history. *Silent Spring* provided the impetus for a ban on DDT—a popular pesticide that concentrated in the food chain, wreaking havoc on birds and other wildlife—and inspired a powerful environmental movement, with landmarks that include the founding of the Environmental Defense Fund in 1967 and the first Earth Day in 1970. Social investors have been an important part of this movement. Outrage over the Exxon Valdez oil spill of 1989 led to the creation of the CERES Principles on environmental practices, and shareholders soon filed resolutions calling on major corporations to adhere to them. A combined effort by shareholder activists and indigenous people persuaded government officials in Québec, Canada, to halt a massive hydroelectric project in 1994. And today, investors are encouraging corporations to cut their greenhouse gas emissions, protect fragile habitats and buy lumber and paper grown in sustainably managed forests. Recently, investors —including my own firm—helped convince JPMorgan Chase—a $1.1 trillion bank with operations in more than 50 countries—to adopt a comprehensive environmental policy. Yet much work remains to be done. In a chilling reminder that a "silent spring" isn't an outdated threat, biologist Bridget Stutchbury, author of *Silence of the Songbirds*, recently wrote in *The New York Times* that our hunger for out-of-season fruits and vegetables may be killing songbirds in Latin America.

In an effort to meet the demand from North America and Europe for a culinary "endless summer," farmers in countries like Guatemala, Honduras and Ecuador are spraying their crops "heavily and repeatedly with a chemical cocktail of dangerous pesticides," as Stutchbury wrote. "Migratory songbirds like bobolinks, barn swallows and Eastern kingbirds are suffering mysterious population declines," she continued, "and pesticides may well be to blame."

What can we do as consumers, as citizens and as investors? Stutchbury urges us to buy organic coffee and organic bananas, and avoid Latin American crops such as melons, green beans, tomatoes, bell peppers and strawberries, which are rarely organically grown. We can ask our government representatives to ensure that labels like "organic" are strict and meaningful. Or, as we cut into our out-of-season tomatoes, peppers and melons, we can thank the hundreds of songbirds who were permanently silenced to bring that produce to our table. It's our choice.

Live off the land

As I was fussing about in the backyard, taking the steps I take each fall in preparation for the winter months, I found myself ruminating about how different my gardening experience is from that of my forebears. Although I'm a lifelong gardener, I am a novice compared with any early settler in Colonial New England.

In March 2004, *The New England Quarterly* published *To Forward Well-Flavored Productions: The Kitchen Garden in Early New England* by James E. McWilliams. It's a treasure trove of basic gardening advice. By extension, it is also a deep dive into what can be accomplished by those seeking self-sufficiency.

By 1660, Colonial New England had evolved into a network of towns and hamlets, each governed through a form of communal meeting, generally at the local church. There was no currency for most of the population and no major industry that employed enough people to create an economic bond like the one we know today. Self-sufficiency, particularly in regards to food, was a simple necessity for survival.

From the article, I learned that the average allotment of land was one acre. On this acre, the family would build a home, perhaps a shelter for animals and other outbuildings, and would grow the crops they would consume that year. This seems impossible to me: Surely an acre was far too little space for the job. Clearly, the early settlers did not need a park space, but even assuming every inch was spent on gardens, could it be true?

Certainly there was a healthy barter system in place. Early records show that women were just as active in commerce as men, trading a bolt of newly woven linen for the construction of a sheep pen or turning a collar for a handful of nails. But when it came to food, trade played a minor role. The growing was what mattered.

The effort required to live off the land was enormous. One early diary tells us that the woman of the house planted turnips and cabbage stumps on May 9; the next day she planted cucumbers and three kinds of squash. Two days after that she planted squash and cucumbers while her husband mended the fence. And this was simply one of the chores she faced each day as she raised her children, cooked, cleaned, made and sewed fabric, and perhaps carried on some sort of trade.

Gardens demand more than plants, and so the man of the house would also be busy, splicing new types of apple, plum, and cherry branches onto established trunks. An acre would probably have four fruit trees, each providing three types of its fruit. The soil was treated with horse manure for trees and cow manure for vegetables. January was a time to destroy nests and sharpen tools. February meant it was time to hack through the frozen earth to plant garlic, potatoes, horseradish, and even cabbage. It was the time to repair walkways and turn the compost heap.

I don't do much in my garden during January, February, or March. In April or May, I have enough to keep my weekend afternoons busy, but it is nothing like what our ancestors took for granted. And when it comes time for harvest, I don't save the seeds and bulbs. There are no baskets of apples in root cellars, nor any carrots. My harvest goes directly into an electric refrigerator, and I don't overly concern myself with using it quickly.

We've lost so much routine knowledge. How to sort the strongest seed to store and use next spring. What sort of soil in what location is best for what sort of vegetable. Using the south-facing wall as a ripening spot and planting fruit against it. Will my children know even less? It is a pleasure to feel my hands in the soil and to sense a connection to the generations that have passed, but I know that precious knowledge is being squandered and that the direct line to the past is being lost. And yet today I read that in a poll of Americans, gardening was named their favorite hobby. It makes me glad, and I hope that this timeworn pastime will continue to instill an appreciation for practical knowledge.

The corn dilemma

As someone who eats cornflakes, I was immediately interested in a headline from a recent *Bloomberg* business article, "U.S. Forced to Import Corn as Shoppers Demand Organic Food." It turns out that our organic demands are a pretty good thing for some small economies in other parts of the world. I learned, for instance, that the value of Romanian corn exports to the U.S. rose to $11.6 million in 2014, from $545,000 the year before. That's a pretty big jump.

What is going on here? Corn is about as American as apple pie. It's one of the crops that grew on our continent before the Europeans arrived. And we certainly grow a lot of it. According to the National Corn Growers Association, we're the largest producer of corn in the world, responsible for 32 percent of the world's crop in the early 2010s. We have 84 million acres of land devoted to corn crops, according to the Environmental Protection Agency, and that corn sells for about $63.9 billion a year.

But apparently big corn growers in America don't want to bother with organic corn. They have their system. They use genetically modified corn that can withstand huge amounts of pesticides without dying; they spray their crops and have no pests. This gives them a high crop yield. It's been going on for years, and the time it would take to reverse course and become qualified organic growers is not, in their view, worth it.

But the demand for organics is growing fast, according to the *Nutrition Business Journal*. Consumer spending on organic foods grew from $11 billion in 2004 to an estimated $27 billion in 2012. It is far and away the largest growth trend in food.

This triggers a whole series of responses in me.

I feel glad that American consumers are supporting farmers in less developed countries who provide a safe and fast-growing product. Their success will raise the standard of living in their communities. I feel sad that we expose our own farmland and consumers to so many pesticides and that it is so profitable to do so. I feel a patriotic sense of disgust that we have given away the healthy corn market. After all, I grew up on stories of Natives teaching Puritans to put fish meat in with the corn to get a better crop. It belongs to us. I feel proud that my organic shopping is contributing to such strong demand. And I feel that our agriculture industry is sort of pathetic in that it fights so hard for outdated and increasingly less desired food production methods.

The shift to organic food consumption is an extremely powerful force for good in the world. As long ago as 1992, a National Cancer Institute review of two dozen epidemiological studies found pesticides to be one of five likely suspects explaining why farmers had elevated risks of developing several forms of cancer. Of course, farmers' exposure levels are much higher than average, so, like the canary in the coal mine, they are the first to feel the effects of pesticides in their environment. That study was 23 years ago. You'd have thought that industry itself might have taken steps to move away from the dangerous ways corporate farming had been growing food, but it took consumers to bring change. As millions of Americans began to seek out organic food, more organic food was grown. For higher-priced items like many fresh vegetables, small family farms have successfully converted to organic production methods. But for large crops like corn, we must go abroad to find what we want.

There was a time in my life when I was not especially fanatical about eating organic. I thought of it as a nice thing, but not a needed thing. My own father gave me a bit of a jump start. He had a business. He purchased eggplants, peeled them, sliced them, dipped them in batter, cooked them, froze them, and sold them in bulk to universities and the like for eggplant Parmesan dinners. One year he decided to supplement the purchase with a crop of his own. So, he asked me if I knew of any organic pesticide he might use for his crop. I was surprised and asked him why he cared. His answer was "This is food. People eat it."

Slowing down fast food

My friends and colleagues know I've been an advocate of the Slow Food movement for many years. Founded in Italy 20 years ago, Slow Food celebrates harvests from small-scale family farms, prepared slowly and lovingly with regard for the health and environment of diners. Slow Food seeks to preserve crop diversity, so the unique taste of "heirloom" apples, tomatoes, and other foods don't vanish from the Earth. I wish everyone would choose to eat this way. The positive effects on the health of our bodies, our local economies, and our planet would be incalculable. Why then do I find myself investing in fast-food companies?

Social investing isn't just about investing in perfect companies. (Perfect companies, it turns out, don't exist.) We seek to invest in companies that are moving in the right direction and listening to their critics. We offer a road map to bring those companies to the next level, step by step. No social standard causes us to reject restaurants, even fast-food ones, out of hand. Although we favor local, organic food, we recognize it isn't available in every community, and is often priced above the means of the average household. Many of us live more than 100 miles from a working farm.

Fast food is a way of life. In America, the average person eats it more than 150 times a year. In 2007, sales for the 400 largest U.S.-based fast-food chains totaled $277 billion, up 7 percent from 2006.

Fast food is a global phenomenon. Major chains and their local competitors have opened branches in nearly every country. For instance, in Greece, burgers and pizza are supplanting the traditional healthy Mediterranean diet of fish, olive oil, and vegetables. Doctors are treating Greek children for diabetes, high cholesterol, and high blood pressure—ailments rarely seen in the past.

The fast-food industry won't go away anytime soon. But in the meantime, it can be changed. And because it's so enormous, even seemingly modest changes can have a big impact. In 2006, New York City banned the use of trans fats (a staple of fast food) in restaurants, and in 2008, California became the first state to do so. When McDonald's moved to non-trans fats for making French fries, the health benefits were widespread.

Another area of concern is fast-food packaging, which causes forest destruction and creates a lot of waste. In the U.S. alone, 1.8 million tons of packaging is generated each year. Fast-food containers make up about 20 percent of litter, and packaging for drinks and snacks adds another 20 percent.

A North Carolina-based organization called the Dogwood Alliance has launched an effort to make fast-food companies reduce waste and source paper responsibly. Through a campaign called No Free Refills, the group is pressing fast-food companies to reduce their impact on the forests of the southern U.S., the world's largest paper-producing region.

They're pushing companies to:

• Reduce the overuse of packaging.

• Maximize the use of 100 percent post-consumer recycled boxboard.

• Eliminate paper packaging from the most biologically important endangered forests.

• Eliminate paper packaging from suppliers that convert natural forests into industrial pine plantations.

• Encourage packaging suppliers to source fiber from responsibly managed forests certified by the Forest Stewardship Council.

• Recycle waste in restaurants to divert paper and other material from landfills.

Will the fast-food companies adopt all these measures overnight? No. But along with similar efforts worldwide, this movement signals that consumers and investors are becoming more conscious of steps they can take toward a better world—beginning with the way they eat.

While my heart will always be with Slow Food, I recognize the fast-food industry can improve and that some companies are ahead of others on that path.

*W*hat the wilderness brings

———— ❖ ————

A recent trip to Southern California brought me within an hour's drive of the famed Joshua Tree National Park, a 1,235-square-mile tract of land overseen by the U.S. National Park Service. The park is shockingly beautiful to someone who, like me, was born and lived their entire life in New England. It contains unusual, even unique features of desert life, and a trip in March, as mine was, offers a heady display of cacti flowering. I found myself deeply moved by the spiritual space that a pristine piece of wilderness creates.

The park has many interesting features, one of which is that this American treasure exists because a wealthy socialite, Minerva Hamilton Hoyt, chose to become an activist, advocating for the preservation of desert spaces. In fact, the American people owe her for the protection of Death Valley National Park and Anza-Borrego Desert State Park as well. It is often the case that as I stumble upon a really special place in America, I hear the same story. One person, frequently someone who gets no personal benefit from his or her actions, becomes passionate about protecting a small corner of the universe and, through that passion, is successful in preserving a location full of marvels for generations to come. And always, government plays a vital role.

It was with great surprise that I watched the news unfold in January 2016. In a spot I'd never heard of, eastern Oregon's Malheur National Wildlife Refuge, a group of individuals gathered to argue that the lands that belong to all citizens, through our National Park Service, ought to be turned over to a handful of ranchers. I immediately felt struck by this reversal of the well-known story of preservation and became curious about the Malheur's founding. It turns out that during the 1880s, many species of American birds had been decimated because their feathers were being used to decorate hats. Ornithologists were alarmed. And in a few short years, George Bird Grinnell founded the Audubon Society and appealed to the president of the United States, Theodore Roosevelt, to set aside lands for the preservation of breeding grounds for native birds. The Malheur became one of these, as it is an important breeding area, especially for the greater sandhill crane.

What got these individuals so riled up in January? I could understand an argument that government-owned property had crowded out ranchers, and that many people feel they need meat, and government ought to free up some land for that purpose. But in fact, the latter is already the case. The Bureau of Land Management manages 155 million acres of land set aside for livestock grazing. It awards leases for ten years at a time. The cost to the rancher is now $2.11 per month for enough forage to keep a cow and her calf alive for a year. In the meantime, the BLM spent $79.9 million in 2014 assuring that the land and water are healthy enough for grazing while collecting $12.1 million in fees. That sort of subsidy to cattle ranchers is pretty impressive.

If ranchers actually receive subsidies to run cattle over public lands, then what was the motivation of those who chose to invade and commandeer a bird sanctuary? They appeared to expect their actions to stimulate others to occupy federal lands. To me, their ideas were quite far-fetched and certainly not desirable. National parks are a treasure for all who walk through them. Each is unique and each is under pressure. Would we even have a clue about what ocean beaches once looked like if we did not have the great national preserves like Anastasia State Park, near St. Augustine, Florida, or the Cape Cod National Seashore? With the pressures for development in Southern California, would a Joshua tree still survive, let alone live in a namesake park?

I've never fallen into the anti-government category; anarchy doesn't appeal to me much. And I've rarely appreciated the government as much as I do when I find myself walking through protected lands, lands waiting for you and me to enter and enjoy. I hope there isn't any more silliness about removing the parks from federal oversight. As fewer and fewer Americans live in close proximity to pristine places, our national parks become more of a treasure, not less. The National Park Service is turning 100 years old this year. Let's use this as a chance to celebrate what wilderness brings to us and recall that the many, working together, have preserved for all an abundance of special spots in this great land of ours.

Profit

Thoughts on People, Planet, & Profit

A (non-) sentimental education

When I was about 15, I learned about stocks and bonds, annual reports, and accounting oversight. Financial education is simple, but people don't know that. And because they don't know enough, they damage themselves and the planet. Here's what I learned.

It began when my grandfather called me for help in the garden. We sliced dahlia bulbs and dug the parts into the ground. As we worked, my grandfather spoke about why he knew how to buy a good stock. He talked about it for quite a while before I said, "I don't really know what a stock is." He was flummoxed. "Why, Amy D. You better come inside so we can discuss this."

Think about the general store in town, my grandfather said. If Mr. Hubbard thinks he might like to open a second general store for his son to run in the next town over, he'll need money. It's expensive to get a store up and running.

Now Mr. Hubbard faces two choices. He can get a loan. When people get loans, they promise to repay them by a certain date. Meanwhile, they pay interest. That's what's called a bond. People put up collateral, maybe the store itself, and it is bonded (or held captive) until the loan is paid off.

The second option is for Mr. Hubbard to find a partner with money who would own a share of the enterprise. The partner would be a shareholder. That means he'd own stock in whatever the store had. The shareholder doesn't get interest, but if the store makes money to spare, that shareholder gets a piece of the profits. That's a dividend.

In my grandfather's house was a stack of what looked like magazines. He said they were annual reports and that every company that sells stock to the public publishes one. He pulled the first one off the stack, flipped to the back and taught me to start there. First, he said, look at the auditor's report. They are all the same. If one is different, that means the auditors don't trust the numbers management is supplying. That would be like calling Mr. Hubbard a liar; you wouldn't invest in a company run by a liar.

We flipped to the front. "That's where the person running the company tells you what the strategy is for the next year or two. You'd better see if you like it. Look for clues that they are getting into riskier business or that they've gotten in over their heads."

As I became an investor, I remembered that to be a good one, you had to find the clues and make your decision. Today I use company reports to find out whether the company's management knows its job is to care for profits, people, and the planet. If it's an airplane company, I want it to have newer, cleaner burning jets and a good safety record. If it's a shampoo company, I want it to have a board diversified in a way that reflects the general public and to advertise fairly. I don't want to see product safety recalls.

When I look at banks, I want to see if they are in the lending business. A lot of them have started doing other work, like insuring portfolios. I find it hard to invest in big American banks, but the ones in Canada are lending. That's why they've been doing better than big American banks lately.

Finding companies that do what they are supposed to do and do it responsibly can prevent problems. Learning a little about what a stock is, what a bond is, and how to decide if you want to invest is well worth the time. You can help yourself by investing for profit. But you can help yourself and others by understanding what a company does right and what it gets wrong. Sunshine is the best disinfectant and responsible investors create the sunlight that shines on the companies. People and planet count on financial systems to provide them with a future. A lot of managers at a lot of companies understand that. To find out which ones do, you have to read the clues. It's not so hard; a 15-year-old kid can do it.

£and ho!

My grandmother taught me to sail. She was a physically and spiritually lovely person with the spunk of a child. She found joy in taking a wooden sailboat out into the wind and chop; she loved the creaking of the wood under strain, the assured threats of knotted lines and rip tides. Now I do, too.

The most important lesson she taught me was that although we cannot affect the wind's strength or direction or the tide's force or stage, we will reach our destination through the proper use of what we can affect: the set of the sails. I remember that when I'm managing investment portfolios in a difficult market.

A couple of columns ago, I spoke of how easy it is to learn basic financial terms. It is also child's play to learn basic financial tactics. First, pick a destination. Boats move because the wind fills the sails and pushes them through the water. Unless you know where you want to end up, you won't set sail in the right direction. Retired people want to outlive their resources; college savings accounts are meant to be spent.

Once your course is set, check for obstacles. The knowledge of what cannot be seen, like underwater rocks, is essential. The enterprise is doomed unless the sailor has done some studying. The investor must do the same. But don't study how to invest; study your resources. How secure is your income? If you suddenly lose your job, how long will you survive on your savings?

After studying the potential for hidden problems, you will want to adjust your approach. Decide on an amount that should stay in the bank, even if it earns little.

That amount is between three months' worth of spending (for those with a secure income flow) and two years' worth. That's a necessary precaution. It doesn't get you there, but it keeps you afloat.

Next, you need a vehicle for your investments. Whether it is an investment manager or a mutual fund family, you cannot launch without faith in the means of transport. I've seen people scatter their assets and keep track of them on a spreadsheet, but that is like sailing a poorly equipped boat. When you are ready to set sail, you do two things: Steer with a tiller to adjust your course and adjust your power by aligning your sails with the wind. With investing, steering is deciding how much to use equities (stocks, venture capital) versus debt (bonds, certificates of deposit, loans). We used to say your age was the percent to have in bonds. If you were 45, you should be 45 percent in bonds. But we live longer, so we can go with our age minus 10. 35 percent in a general quality bond fund and 65 percent in a general stock fund is the simple answer.

How much do you save? Your budget needs to include a line item for saving. Good savers have an automatic withdrawal from their bank accounts or paychecks. Let's say you are the 45-year-old above and the vessel is a mutual fund family or a 401k plan, then every month a specific amount will be contributed, 35 percent to a bond fund and 65 percent to a stock fund. My grandmother would giggle, but her words were warnings. "Ready about" means: Get ready to alter course and move the nose of the boat through the source of the wind. As the boat shifts, the wind will force the sail to move across the deck. But sails moving across the deck can knock people overboard. "Hard alee" tells you how she'll move the boat through the wind. She'll shove the tiller toward the side of the boat farthest from the wind. The sail will sweep; the boat may flop. Get ready.

Altering course is what you have to do when things go wrong. So, make changes deliberately. Don't fear them. But don't underestimate them either. Morningstar estimates that a dollar invested in 1926 would have grown to $2,982 in 2010 in the stock market. But if you missed the best 39 months, you would have only $19.05 (less than treasury bills).

With these rules, you can sidestep most of the financial mistakes people make. One: Set a destination. Two: Prepare for obstacles. Three: Find a seaworthy ship. Four: Allocate assets. Five: Commit to regular infusions. And finally, approach course alterations seriously. Follow this advice and you will be a better investor.

*M*edicine for economies

We often overlook what makes an economy healthy. I read stories about reducing the deficit, spurring on businesses, rewarding the job creators, but none address America's dependence on consumer spending for its gross domestic product (GDP). Debates rage over what we count, but most sources claim that more than 70 percent of our GDP comes from consumer spending, compared to 55 percent during the 1950s.

For many Americans, the 1950s were the glory years. We baby boomers grew up playing with fewer toys, living in much smaller houses, eating much smaller meals, and we generally view the time as patriotic and happy. Whatever the exact proportion attributable to business and government (the other two drivers of GDP) during the 1950s, it was, to the satisfaction of most economists, clearly larger than it is today. Yet as a nation we have taken a number of steps that have left our economy ever more dependent on consumption.

What big forces rolled back contributions of business and government? I think the root causes are overlooked.

First, back in 1954, just over a third of the U.S. workforce belonged to a union. This meant that business had to spend more, which upped its contribution and made consumers wealthier—thereby also upping consumers' contributions. Further, unions trained their members through apprenticeship programs, so businesses had a steady supply of capable and qualified workers, the lack of which is often a problem now for businesses looking to hire. Today, 12 percent of the workforce is in a union. Our workers receive a smaller share of the corporate spending budget, so profits rise but spending does not.

The second cause, a shift in the American psyche, is harder to quantify. Saving has fallen off, while spending has become respectable. It may be that we feel pulled to spend by the advertising that bombards us, but it is also true that we no longer honor the hardworking, simple-living, solid-saving person. Perhaps the availability of credit lulls us into thinking the rainy day will never come. When I was quite young, a man told me that of course he could afford a better car, but being wasteful wasn't Christian. Wow. Even if you substitute "a good person" for "Christian," that's a rare sentiment today.

A third factor is the influence of Wall Street on corporations. While in the 1950s top executives were paid 20 times what average workers received, today that figure is 204 times. This pay differential is generally granted as a reward for stock performance—the theory is you want the CEO's interest to be in sync with the investors'. Good stock performance is the result of two factors: Rising corporate earnings and a larger profit margin. Spending now on something that might pay off in five years might help future CEOs but doesn't help now; stretching out maintenance expenses or cutting quality does. Average corporate profit margins during the 1950s were in the high 20 percent range; today they are in the high 30s. That's nice for shareholders and executive bonuses but lousy for growing the economy.

Then there's government. Government spending is dependent on two factors. The U.S. government must have the money to spend (collected via either tax revenues or borrowing), and it must have permission to spend, granted by Congress. Records from the Office of Management and Budget show a slight creep in spending of about 1 percent of GDP since the 1950s. The big contributor is healthcare costs, but although the Affordable Care Act might bring government spending (relative to businesses and consumers) more in line with the 1950s, it still hasn't come close to taking up the slack left by lagging business spending.

What's needed to grow the economy? Since corporations are unlikely to shift their executive incentives, perhaps we need to levy an "alternative tax" on these corporations. Ronald Reagan introduced this tax, which requires individuals to pay at least a base tax, loopholes or not. But the same isn't true for corporations.

We could eventually train and incentivize saving, but in the short term that will dampen the economy. Corporations could be given incentives to contribute more, though it is hard to see how. But government can spend right away. An alternative tax on corporate profits would make that possible. The ever-growing profit margins among companies aren't good enough for Americans—the nation needs the cash.

Thoughts on People, Planet, & Profit

What we know can't hurt us

*T*he Massachusetts shore has lured visitors and new residents to its fabled beaches and healthy lifestyle for generations. There you find bicyclists along the paths, older folks practicing tai chi on the village squares, and strong swimmers plying the waterways. But in this wholesome spot, women kept noticing that their friends were getting sick, dying. Breast cancer is practically an epidemic on Cape Cod. Some women began asking why. The cancer zones seemed to follow water sources. These women gathered data on the release of poisons in the region and began to trace them. They were able to gather this data because of an unusual law. The Toxic Release Inventory mandates that facilities track and report on their release of certain hazardous materials.

This story is still playing itself out, but if the women learn why their friends are dying, it will be because of disclosure. Transparency is essential. Once the Sullivan Principles mandated reporting on progress toward equality in South Africa, it became obvious that there was no progress, and civil society took action.

Yet today, virtually no mandatory non-investor-driven disclosure exists. Particularly in the U.S., corporate disclosure has grown out of reforms that date back to the 1930s, when it was essential that investors be reassured that they were being treated fairly.

This simple notion has led to unanticipated consequences. An industry of enormous proportions grew up with the sole purpose of allowing investors to evaluate the prices of financial instruments and trade them, with the idea that corporate interests must supersede the interests of other stakeholders.

Financial impacts on the taxpayer, for example, are hidden. Today, society finds Wall Street pitted against Main Street about where to allocate costs and where to realize benefits.

This takes us to the role of responsible investors. We recognize the importance of mandated disclosure and seek to demand it wherever we can. But the failure of government to move quickly to institute it is no reason for us to sit still. We are not value-neutral about what will benefit us, and we demand that our investments meet at least basic stakeholder standards in order to indicate progress.

By moving forward ourselves, we have built the template for future legislation, while establishing the databases that even today help grassroots organizations sift through suspected causes of harm and pinpoint their sources.

The application of social criteria to investments is widely misunderstood but all-important. We cannot know today what needs it will meet, but we do know that the world needed data before it brought so much pressure to bear that 27 million people were given the vote in South Africa. We know that the toxic data that the women of Cape Cod are studying may save lives for centuries to come.

————————◆●◆————————

And we know that when accountability is mandated, behavior improves. Nothing has been as powerful as socially responsible investing in moving disclosure standards forward.

It is a legacy of which we can be proud.

————————◆●◆————————

*A*sking questions, changing companies

In 1970, *The New York Times Magazine* published an article by economist Milton Friedman, the title of which elegantly summarized its most salient point: "The Social Responsibility of Business Is to Increase its Profits." In the years since, he and many others have continued to assert that there's no need for investors to consider social and environmental factors, adding that the misguided pursuit of "corporate social responsibility" completely missed the point of free-market capitalism.

Though "free market" ideologues continue to make this argument, the business world has changed markedly. It's widely accepted these days that corporate social responsibility (a concept so institutionalized it's known by its acronym: CSR) involves far more than maximizing earnings. This change has come about mainly because investors have begun to consider social and environmental factors seriously when they make their investment decisions.

Like so many people, I prefer to invest in companies whose business practices promote human dignity and environmental protection. We do this because companies that respect the environment and their employees tend to be well-managed, and over the long term this can translate into strong financial performance.

Every business has an impact far beyond the CEO's office, and faces a multitude of decisions relating to social and environmental issues. When investors incorporate that impact, we build an infrastructure for understanding and evaluating corporate behavior.

But this isn't a passive process of evaluation. By asking the hard questions and communicating with companies about the ways we expect them to behave, we help redefine the role they play in our society.

When communities were devastated because of decisions made by executives in the past, protests and fines often prompted action. But did those executives hear from their shareholders—their bosses? No. Shareholders only asked how much money they made that quarter.

Social investors are now setting the standard for social and environmental reporting and performance, much as an earlier generation of analysts set expectations and created standards for corporate financial reporting. Today, thousands of companies around the world respond to our questions about their business decisions. They publish CSR reports, maintain websites touting their ethics, and provide data to back up their claims.

Many would say this is simply public relations, or "greenwashing." And some of it is. But these reports are also something far more important. They're conversation-starters. They're accountability tools.

When a CEO signs off on a financial report, she asks questions. "Why did our numbers improve here, but not here? What will next year's report look like? Can we do better next time?" If she doesn't ask, there's sure to be a member of the board, or an angry shareholder, who will.

Every time a CEO signs off on a sustainability report, you can be sure the same kinds of questions are being asked. "What can I tell the press about this child labor violation on page 23? How do I explain this decrease in toxic emissions to analysts? Can we double that next year?"

Milton Friedman, who died in 1996 at the age of 94, lived long enough to observe, if not appreciate, a sea change in corporate culture. After all these years, smart companies came to understand that the social responsibility of business means so much more than increasing profits. Shareholders are asking the companies they own to account for the way they treat people and the planet. And if CEOs don't provide answers, they'll hear about it.

Carrying the torch

As I write this column, the Olympic torch is making its way around the world, heading to the Olympic Games in Beijing. For the runners who carry the torch, and many others who plan to compete in China, the torch and the Olympics represent the purity of athletic competition, which is or should be above politics. Others, however, view the Olympics as an opportunity for the host country to burnish its image and sweep abuses under the rug. Protesters who want freedom in Tibet, or who object to human rights violations in China, have met the torch with shouts and placards and sometimes scuffles.

Opinions on how to promote human rights in China and elsewhere are wide-ranging—but that's not the subject of this column. Whatever one's position on this summer's Olympic Games, the torch itself is a potent symbol for the moral questions that face all of us every day. And the important thing to note about this symbol is that it isn't standing still. It's moving.

The idea that change is the only constant has become a cliché. But it's true. On topics as diverse as sweatshop labor and global warming, powerful trends are already in motion. We can no longer opt out of making decisions on the major issues of our time. Not to decide is to be carried away, for better or worse, on the wave of decisions made by others. As historian Howard Zinn put it in the title of his memoir, *You can't be neutral on a moving train.*

Even an everyday matter like the food you eat has far-reaching implications. Are your vegetables grown without putting toxic pesticides and chemical fertilizers into the ground? Are your fruits shipped by carbon-spewing airplanes from distant continents? Do the workers who harvest your coffee beans earn enough to feed their kids? When we invest, we face questions, each of which requires us to decide whether to be carried along with the mainstream or to move in a different direction.

Those of us who consider ourselves socially responsible investors don't want to profit from products and practices that undermine human dignity or harm the environment. We also think it's reasonable to believe that by selecting companies with positive social and environmental records we can avoid those most affected by strikes, boycotts, and penalties, and benefit from forward-looking management that can translate into strong financial performance over the long term.

The incentive to get off the train of international finance is strong, because it appears to be hurtling toward a cliff when it should be racing into a brighter future. That's impossible. It's our hopes and dreams, in the form of our college and retirement savings, that fuel this train. It's our responsibility to use the power of our decisions to switch the train onto a different track before it's too late.

The "big lie" inherent in traditional investment advice is that this is somebody else's business. It's our business, and our shared future. We need to apply not just traditional standards like return-on-investment and price-to-earnings ratios, but even more traditional standards of right and wrong—and seek out the information about which companies are meeting those standards.

Getting that information means asking questions, not passively analyzing the usual corporate reports. Sometimes asking the right question can cause company directors to change their approaches or help start a conversation about the way companies should behave.

To invest in this way—consciously, taking responsibility for the impact of our money in the world—can be the first step toward creating more awareness in every aspect of our lives and becoming willing to make the decisions that will shape our world. Little by little, but virtually every day, we're beginning to see a new horizon down the track.

Localism takes hold

One of the truly humiliating experiences of aging is getting to see just how wrong you can be. I was a big fan of David Korten's book, *Making Democracy Work*, when it was first published in 1995. When it was reissued in 2001 with new concepts added, I bought and read it at once. My response: "God bless the man; he is a hopeless dreamer."

How wrong I was. In his re-released edition, Korten argued that only a vibrant and concerted movement to celebrate and support locally owned businesses could sustain a healthy economic life for most of us. He wrote that although large corporations are good at selling large quantities of a product, they squash the neighborhood vendor and fail to provide the local basketball team with bus money. I agreed with that much. But what I could not envision was that people would shift their habits to support locally owned businesses and locally sourced products. That just seemed too farfetched.

But this is a new world, and localism, as it is called, has taken hold. As I pass a farm stand in South Carolina, the "certified South Carolina produce sold" sign urges me in. As I walk to the subway stop in my neighborhood, I pass five "locally owned and operated" signs in windows. In Kentucky, I see "Kentucky Proud" signs to announce the local nature of the business inside. Even at the large chain supermarket where I shop, the signs for "locally grown" loom over vegetables.

This is an important trend. We always had the tourist who insisted on Maine lobster or Vermont maple syrup to enrich their traveling experience, more as a memento than a movement. This is something else. The shopper at the locally owned pharmacy is saying that they get it, that they choose to support the local family that has, in turn, been serving the community, supporting the local elementary school spelling bee, and keeping the developmentally disabled son of a neighbor employed stacking shelves. And if the toothpaste costs 20 cents more (simply because the local pharmacist can't benefit from scale the way the majors can), the customer doesn't see it as a rip off, but as a fair trade.

Some years ago, I wrote about the Slow Food movement, whose advocates urge us to source locally, organically, and humanely. They ask us to prepare traditional recipes and to take the time to enjoy the meal. I wrote that it was a subversive trend. While fun, it taught us about what it was not, and it was not industrial agri-business. It helped remind us that there was something precious in the simpler, older ways. Like Slow Food, localism teaches us something about what it is not. It teaches us to look more broadly at the ecosystem within which we get goods and services, and to shop in a way that leads more directly to the creation of a community in which we want to live.

Localism seems to have taken hold because it speaks to something fundamental about the way humans want to live. We want to feel as though we are part of a community, whether it is our block in the big city or the rural county we call home. Our communities offer resources to finance our lives, to allow us to enjoy dignity, common respect, and companionship with our shopkeepers, our public servants, and our neighbors. These resources don't easily grow out of minimum wage jobs at big box stores, but they are immediately tangible at the local market where we stop and chat about the new stoplight in town as we pick up a carton of milk.

As I think about the larger implications of localism, I see nothing but positives. It isn't like being a fan of your hometown team, fostering resentment and competition. Localism in South Carolina isn't better or worse than localism in Massachusetts. I enjoy the shared commitment to community that localism means everywhere I find it. Oddly, going local seems to be a way of making us all part of something big.

I keep hoping I'll become wise enough to recognize a great thought when I see it, but I'm still waiting. Meanwhile, I'll have to satisfy myself with a quiet apology to David Korten for ever having thought he was a fluffy, softhearted soul instead of the visionary he is.

The slow road to growth

On May 6, 2010, the world of Wall Street went crazy. A sudden frenzy of selling began. Fine blue chip stocks plummeted to levels dramatically below their opening prices. The Dow Jones Industrial Index fell by more than 1,000 points in about half an hour. Volume more than doubled. Traders began frantically searching for a reason. Had there been a nuclear accident? Could the President have been shot? Eventually, it became clear; nothing had happened.

But while there may have been no reason for the drop, there was a cause: high-frequency computer (sometimes called algorithmic) trading. Computers make decisions faster than people do, so it had been only a matter of time before Wall Street firms started depending on them. By using sophisticated algorithms, computers can assess numerous tidbits of information, determine a course of action, and execute it in less time than it takes to blink an eye.

How bad was it? Well, *The Wall Street Journal* reported that shares of consulting company Accenture traded at $39.98 at 2:46 p.m., $38 at 2:47, and one cent at 2:49 p.m. By 2:50 p.m., the stock was back up to $39.51. That is nuts. That is a casino.

Responsible investors have long argued for greater regulation of financial markets and for a greater connection between securities trading and human well-being. We argue that finance is only there to grease the wheels of commerce and that if it fails in this prime purpose, finance needs to change. But recently, a new school of thought is emerging to pursue this argument to a much further degree: the Slow Money movement.

Slow Money is a very simple idea. "Our goal: a million Americans investing one percent of their assets in local food systems ... within a decade," according to the website. Slow Money argues that the reason we have a system of money is to provide ourselves with sustainable and pleasant lives. Core to this realization is the support of sustainable local food sources. And so we can once again know our butcher, baker, and furniture makers, all the while eating much more healthily without degrading the Earth.

High-impact investing can take many forms. It can be a deposit in a community development bank or credit union, which makes money available to lend for high impact in underserved communities. A few organic farming cooperatives and fair trade groups sell preferred stock to support themselves. Some venture capital pools focus on newer, greener businesses. A network of green builders has begun meeting. Financial leaders are discovering that these ideas, which have been developing separately, are part of a larger philosophy, the Slow Money concept.

I often speak of the world of financiers as being similar to a set of horses dragging a stagecoach as they stampede across the landscape. It really doesn't matter where these beasts end up; those on board are doomed. It is only through an orderly movement in a pre-determined direction that the results will be good.

How do you get a set of runaway horses to behave? In the old cowboy movies, the hero would ride up, grab the lead horse by the harness, and moderate the pace and direction. In fact, this is my goal for socially responsible investments. I hope that our actions influence the behavior of financial firms and lead to a better way. I hope our actions bring the passengers on that coach (the family of humankind) to an appropriate destination.

Where does Slow Money fit in all this? It reminds us that in the end, a pleasant experience as we travel through life is more than just enough; it is a goal to be celebrated. If you can afford it, why not invest innovatively at the local level? One percent would make a world of difference.

So now, when I read the financial pages and learn that today the market is up despite weakness in the euro and yesterday the market was down because of weakness in the euro, I can smile. I know that an ever-increasing number of people are choosing the slow road. Slow Food came first, the antidote to fast food. Slow Cities then introduced the antidote to crowded hubs. Now Slow Money arrives to allow us to reconsider the way we invest even beyond responsible investing, right down to the local level.

The buck starts here

As a student of the stock market in particular, and therefore the economy, I find sometimes the simplest lessons are the most often overlooked. Common sense tidbits clearly point to actions the nation ignores. As we try to dig ourselves out of the financial crisis, it is important to focus on these. I'll be pointing out the obvious, and I'll start with the importance of redistributing income and wealth.

Now, remember your Economics 101 college course. There is such a thing as a multiplier effect. The purchase of a tombstone (an item that does not require a system of repairs and multiple uses) is not as good for the overall economy as the purchase of a similarly priced computer, which will require many purchases of electricity, Internet access, software, and peripherals to maintain its efficacy.

Buying a $75 pair of shoes doesn't create the same level of economic stimulation as buying a $50 pair of shoes and a $25 bag of groceries. The first scenario helps roughly identical players as does the purchase of $50 shoes. Buying shoes and groceries helps the infrastructure of the grocery supplier as well as the shoe vendor.

Next, recall that the economy in the U.S. is between two-thirds and three-quarters reliant on consumer spending, depending on who does the estimating. Ideally, this means that public policy should be single-minded in its pursuit of new consumers; that is, getting money into the hands of those who will buy the less expensive pair of shoes and some groceries.

I'm not the only one pointing this out. The U.S. Congressional Budget Office reviewed estimated output multipliers of each of the major provisions of the stimulus bill. They use a range of low to high. The best bang for the buck are federal purchases; next are transfers to states; next are transfer payments to individuals through food stamps, unemployment compensation, health assistance, and the like. This came in as only slightly less valuable as federal and state spending and more than twice as useful as payments to retirees, tax cuts for higher income people, or extension of first-time homebuyer credits. I repeat: More than twice as economically beneficial.

Economic policymakers should be adamant about getting money into the hands of the lowest wage earners. From a purely economic point of view, it does not matter whether the recipient earns this money or receives it as a gift. All this is to say, we are a long way, as a consumption-based economy, from creating policies that support us.

You may be asking about the stronger multipliers, government and state spending. Did you know that according to U.S. Department of Labor statistics, the federal government, excluding the postal service, is the nation's largest employer, employing roughly 2 million civilian employees, the vast majority of whom work outside the Washington, D.C., area? Government spending is by definition a job-creation program.

When I began working in finance, we were taught that purchasing stocks (in American companies; others were not available) was a proxy for purchasing the economic might of our nation. Today that might has faded. The reason it has faded is that we are not deliberate about creating new consumers of the right kind.

Let's start spreading the word. Our self-interest, indeed the nation's economic well-being, starts with creating more people who can spend, even at the risk of creating fewer people who can spend billions.

"Economic policymakers should be adamant about getting money into the hands of the lowest wage earners."

Credit shouldn't cost this much

*P*eople often say to me, "What's next? What are you mad about?" Today, my answer is plastic cards. Credit cards and bank ATM cards were created to help people. I'm old enough to remember pulling out my checkbook and two forms of identification whenever I made a non-cash purchase. It was tiresome to stand in line behind other customers and wait as they flipped to the page where the running tally was kept and noted what was left in the checking account. Bank cards and credit cards, along with the electronic infrastructure to support them, make my life better and the store owner's simpler. But the thrill is gone. These cards are ripping people off and it makes me mad.

According to Consumers Union (CU), the large American consumer advocacy group, banks collect an estimated $7.98 billion in fees from overdrafts triggered by debit and ATM transactions. That's because rather than notifying the consumer that a particular transaction will overdraw the account, the banks eagerly allow it. They argue that it's a service, but I say it's a forced expense. After all, nearly half the people polled by CU assumed their banks would deny a debit transaction or allow it to go through without a charge—until they found out otherwise the hard way.

Credit card abuse is also rampant. Fees, not interest, now account for 39 percent of the revenue for credit card issuers, according to R.K. Hammer, a bank card advisory firm. One example of predatory practices is called double cycle billing. This happens when a credit card holder pays interest on money that's already paid back. Let's say you owe $1,000 at the beginning of a billing cycle and pay $500 toward the balance. Under double cycle billing you'll be charged interest on the full $1,000 in the next cycle.

Thank goodness, regulators are taking note. The European Commission took credit card executives to task for exorbitant fees, and in April, MasterCard agreed to lower fees to roughly 38 percent of the previous levels (in Europe only). MasterCard didn't do this willingly and has taken the matter to the courtroom. In the U.S., Congress is debating regulations aimed at unfair practices. As the European Commission was acting, the U.S. Senate Banking Committee approved a bill that would stop many such practices. The bill would require 45 days advance notice of interest rate hikes and end double cycle billing.

Responsible investors are at the forefront of the challenge. We've taken the lead with credit card companies, as we did with predatory lenders in the housing markets 10 years ago. In the fall of last year, a coalition of investors affiliated with the Interfaith Center on Corporate Responsibility, including Domini Impact Investments, filed shareholder resolutions that will appear on the ballots of the three biggest U.S. credit card companies: Citigroup, JPMorgan Chase, and Bank of America. These resolutions call on these multinational firms' boards of directors to assess the extent to which they use predatory practices. If you hold shares in these companies, please consider voting for these proposals. This group has also engaged in dialogue with American Express, Discover, Capital One, and Wells Fargo.

There's much to admire about plastic money. Credit cards offer entrepreneurs with little or no collateral a way to finance the start-up of their small businesses. They certainly allow the young to build a credit history, making a mortgage possible one day. But the shift from making money by floating a loan to making money by charging fees on actions the consumer didn't even know could be taken (like overspending an account) is destroying any goodwill I might harbor for the industry. As was the case with predatory mortgages, predatory card practices are hurting people and squelching hope.

Investors of goodwill, take note.

Democratic capitalism

L ast year, when Muhammad Yunus won the Nobel Peace Prize, millions of people around the world learned of the miracles that banks serving the poor could deliver. It was a well-deserved honor for Yunus, and a great reminder of what microloans and other slight tweaks to "business as usual" can mean to hundreds of thousands of disenfranchised people. Yunus' Grameen Bank is a marvelous example of the potential of community lending, the third leg of the stool for socially responsible investing. (The others are setting standards for what shares we will buy and entering into dialogue with companies we own.) For large populations around the globe, "the triumph of capitalism" has meant no improvement to personal well-being. Even in wealthy nations, large pockets of poverty are scattered throughout crowded and crumbling inner cities and hard-hit agricultural areas. Around the globe, many people are able and willing to work, but have little opportunity.

Access to capital is an essential component of building healthy communities. But capital is not always available to the poor. Banks are driven by the desire to be ever more profitable. Since a $600 loan and a $6 million loan take about the same effort from the bank, and have a vastly different impact on the bottom line, the bank opts to eliminate smaller customers.

In addition, poor people seeking a loan often appear suspicious or quirky to bankers. For example, let's look at the case of a mobile home park where an old couple running the operation wants to retire by selling the land. Between them, the owners of these mobile homes may have enough income to buy the land with a loan to be paid back over a reasonable period of time. But banks don't lend to new co-operative ventures. They lend to a person or a corporation with good credit. Since no single person living in the mobile home park can guarantee the payments, there can be no loan.

Community-oriented financial institutions have come about as an answer to this problem. Such institutions may be a bank (or a bank branch) dedicated to making loans that boost the community and alleviate poverty. It may be a credit union, created perhaps by a church or community group, that loans money only to its own members and only for the purpose of building healthier neighborhoods. It may even be a non-profit group, set up to borrow from caring people and lend to those in need.

Support for these kinds of community-development financial institutions is one of the ways in which sustainable or socially responsible investing can be approached. At Domini Impact Investments, we have a fund that purchases bonds, backing up community institutions that make microcredit loans globally; we purchase insured deposits that support poor populations; we even use activist tools to help the community-development world.

Community-development loans have an important place in socially responsible investment portfolios, allowing investors to participate directly in relieving poverty and—unlike philanthropy—enabling them to keep their money even after using it this way. Most important, such loans offer evidence that finance can be used to alleviate poverty and create universal human dignity. Nowhere is the connection stronger than it is when investors support these grassroots lending organizations, be they microcredit institutions like Grameen Bank in Bangladesh or community-building groups like Latino Community Credit Union or the Self Help Credit Union, both in North Carolina.

ℬroken homes

A cross the U.S., people are losing their homes. In just the month of July, more than a quarter-million American households received a foreclosure-related filing, telling them to pay up or be put out on the street. Numbers like these fail to convey the oceans of human heartache they represent. The so-called "subprime crisis" is really a story about Americans' homes and the broken system within which we buy and try to hold on to them. There's plenty of blame to go around. Some certainly belongs to speculators planning to "flip" houses in a rising market. These buyers are partly to blame for the run-up in prices. Some belongs to homebuyers who took advantage of loans without background checks, which allowed them to lie about their income and assets. Other borrowers didn't think about the possibility of rising payments, or didn't fully understand the terms of their loans.

Much more blame goes to dishonest mortgage salesmen and their company CEOs. But the root causes of this crisis lie in yet another corruption of capitalism, in which the only value seems to be that of the quick buck.

Not many years ago, America's home-finance system looked much like the one portrayed in the 1946 film classic *It's a Wonderful Life*. Workers and middle-class people put their savings (yes, back then Americans actually saved) into local banks closely supervised by regulators. When community members were ready to buy houses, they'd go to the same places for their mortgages.

The relationship between the banks and their customers was long term, and all parties were invested in the homes and the communities. These banks' survival depended on the care with which they made loans, and on their borrowers' ability to pay. *It's a Wonderful Life* allowed a bank president to look into the future: into a world with no caring banks, into a town's demise. It showed how those local financial institutions were the backbones of their communities, and suggested the social breakdown that would occur if they were no longer around.

Six decades later, home finance works very differently. As the banking sector consolidated, local banking institutions disappeared. Deposit accounts and mortgage loans became commodities, sold on the basis of interest rates rather than service quality, local presence, or long-term relationship.

Quasi-governmental home-finance institutions like Fannie Mae and Freddie Mac, designed to make home ownership easier for middle-class Americans, turned many banks into little more than loan-origination companies. The mortgages they issued were packaged and sold to other investors. Lenders stopped worrying about whether loans would get repaid, focused as they were on their initial sales commissions.

Meanwhile, the feds eliminated crucial government oversight, and the Federal Reserve embarked on a policy of easy credit for all. Investment banks used their massive brainpower to structure esoteric ways to package and sell mortgage loans. And millions of people saw the easy money, heard the sales pitches, ignored the fine print, believed the housing market would keep rising forever, and signed on the dotted line.

The salesperson focuses on his commission, the CEO or investment banker on her bonus. The politician focuses on his ideology (or on winning elections). The business community pushes for less oversight, less regulation, and less responsibility as it maximizes profits.

There is, however, another way, and it can be seen in communities across the U.S. (Under the heading of microfinance, it's also an important trend in other parts of the world.) Community banks, credit unions, and other community development financial institutions (CDFIs) are lending money the old-fashioned way—in the context of long-term relationships between borrowers and their communities. In my next column, I'll take a look at how CDFIs are addressing the foreclosure crisis, and showing us a model for more sustainable financial services.

A different kind of home security

W hile its influence has touched the world, the financial crisis created by subprime mortgage lending has its roots firmly planted in the U.S. Because the crisis serves as a warning to other countries, America's efforts to respond to it may provide useful guidance.

In last month's column, I looked at the massive wave of foreclosures in the U.S. and the broken system of home ownership that made this crisis possible and even inevitable. This month, I'd like to highlight some aspects of what's being done to help homeowners minimize its devastating effects.

Governments, employers, and community development financial institutions (CDFIs) have all taken action in different ways. In the U.S., governments have acted on local and national levels. A bill to help borrowers at risk of foreclosure refinance their mortgages gained broad support in Congress, although it was delayed by controversy over whether and how to rescue the major mortgage lenders Fannie Mae and Freddie Mac. A program launched by the city of Philadelphia, Pennsylvania, seeks to prevent foreclosures by requiring officials to negotiate with lenders to restructure loans and allow borrowers to keep their homes. In Baltimore, Maryland, the Belair-Edison Neighborhood Initiative reaches out to homeowners with high-interest or adjustable-rate mortgages (ARMs), providing free counseling and access to more affordable alternatives.

A few U.S. firms have also addressed the problem. As *The Wall Street Journal* reported last summer, "A handful of companies—from small manufacturers to large companies like home-financing behemoth Fannie Mae—are offering assistance, such as interest-free loans, grants, and support in securing rental properties. They're also beefing up their employee-assistance programs, or EAPs, and adding more educational seminars on personal finance."

CDFIs play a big role. Community development is often neglected in social investing, but recent events underline its importance.

ShoreBank, one of the biggest and oldest CDFIs in the U.S., developed its Rescue Loan Program in response to foreclosures in Chicago, Illinois, and elsewhere. Bank executives found that about 10,000 homeowners in its priority neighborhoods would qualify to replace their ARMs with 30-year fixed-rate mortgages. Among them were the Villareal family, who saved their house on Chicago's West side. As Rudy Villareal said, "I tell everyone about ShoreBank. I just couldn't disappoint my son. He was so excited about having our own home."

Self-Help Credit Union, another CDFI, works with a non-profit organization called the Center for Responsible Lending. The Center has concentrated its efforts on legislative change, testifying in Congress to allow judges to revise the terms of some loans, holding Wall Street companies responsible for buying predatory loans and barring products such as "option" ARMs.

While pushing for tighter regulations, the Center argues that state laws protecting consumers should be left in place, since states have more flexibility to address local conditions and respond to the tactics of predatory lenders.

This economic crisis will take time and work to get through. Addressing even one aspect requires the efforts of many institutions. Community development banks and credit unions, with their roots in the communities hardest hit by foreclosure, are uniquely positioned to help soften the blow.

Trial by corporation

As an advocate of socially responsible investing, I study companies. One good source of understanding is a review of the number of times and ways they are sued. This helps me understand a company's culture. If I see a lawsuit over a worker's death, I don't think about it much.

But if I see several lawsuits about worker deaths, I see a pattern. That pattern, along with other information—on innovation, environmental remediation, or personnel policies—helps me decide if I want to own the company's stock.

Companies don't want lawsuits. You can hardly blame them. But society needs protection, and lawsuits are how we protect ourselves. One of the smartest rules we have is that we punish companies by charging them more than their unlawful acts cost those who have been harmed. Punitive damages keep them focused on the risk of behaving poorly. Our Bill of Rights contains the right to trial by jury. It is fundamental to our nation's DNA. The courtroom is the only place where an ordinary person stands on equal footing with the powerful. And if a jury of 12 determines that the ordinary person was harmed by neglectful (or worse) behavior on the part of a company, that company has to pay in two ways. First, it must repay for the harm caused. Next, it must pay an extra amount, large enough to discourage other companies from the behavior that led to the harm.

How are companies trying to put an end to trials? They call it "tort reform," and the tactic is to trivialize the good work of citizens serving on a jury. I am indebted to the HBO documentary show *Hot Coffee* for bringing to my attention the profoundly un-American campaign that so-called tort reform represents.

The attacks got a big boost when former U.S. President Ronald Reagan famously belittled a janitor who had lost a leg, saying, "In California, a man was using a public telephone booth to place a call. An alleged drunk driver careened down the street, lost control of his car, and crashed into the phone booth. Now, it's no surprise that the injured man sued. But you might be startled to hear whom he sued: The telephone company and associated firms!"

Now, wait a minute. Why shouldn't he sue the phone company? The victim lost his leg because the door of the telephone booth jammed. A witness testified that the victim had been trying to escape the phone booth prior to the car's appearance. The phone company hadn't repaired the door in spite of several complaints. Furthermore, the placement of the booth was dangerous. It had been hit by a car 20 months earlier but hadn't been moved. By the way, the victim tried to sue the driver, but the police lost the driver's blood alcohol test. At any rate, the bar at which she drank settled for $25,000.

Then there's the woman who spilled coffee on herself and got $4 million. Seventy-nine-year-old Stella Liebeck was sitting in the passenger seat of a parked car. She wanted to add sugar to a cup of coffee. With the paper cup held between her knees, she pulled the lid open, spilling the cup on her lap, suffering third-degree burns to her thighs, buttocks, and groin. Two years of medical treatment followed. She asked the restaurant chain to cover her costs, but they declined.

Pre-trial discovery showed that the coffee, by company mandate, was heated to 180 to 190 degrees Fahrenheit, a temperature that produces third-degree burns in two seconds, and that the company had received more than 700 similar complaints. The jurors awarded personal damages of $200,000.

The jury decided to punish the company by awarding a payment that represented about two days worth of the restaurant chain's coffee profits, or $2.7 million. The case was settled for less than $600,000. These and a dozen other cases were reported as silly lawsuits in which silly jurors had handed out princely sums. Talk show hosts pummeled jurors and victims relentlessly. Public relations, paid for by big business, turned what should have been an affirmation of the value of trials into an attack on lawyers and the law; the real story is that companies don't care that juries date back to ancient Athens and were made law by the U.S. Constitution.

Corporate America doesn't want ordinary citizens to have as much power as they do. This is the dismantling of a great American tradition. The next time you hear about a dumb lawsuit, take the time to find out what happened. An awful lot of the time, it is the story of an ordinary American trying to get on with his or her life.

Thoughts on People, Planet, & Profit

Get invested
in change

*T*he foggy coastal rainforest of British Columbia is home to mountain goats, bald eagles, and a rare species of black bear. Of every 10 bear cubs born, one is white or cream-colored. They are known as Spirit Bears. Like other rainforests, this one helps protect the Earth against global warming by absorbing carbon in the form of CO_2, which prevents the carbon from being released into the atmosphere.

Most people would agree this is a poor place for logging. Yet Kimberly-Clark— the world's largest manufacturer of tissue products, including Kleenex, and one of the biggest buyers of wood products—admitted after previous denials that some of the wood fiber it buys has come from logs cut from trees growing along the coast of British Columbia.

This spring, Kimberly-Clark took an important step toward responsible forestry practices. The company agreed it would give preference to wood fiber certified by the Forest Stewardship Council (FSC), a group widely recognized for its independence, transparency, and inclusiveness. This is good news for the environment, but it also underlines the importance of a critical tool used by responsible investors—a tool that is under threat.

Shareholder resolutions, particularly those that focus on environmental, social, or governance issues, have long been a thorn in the side of corporate management. Limiting or eliminating the ability to bring such resolutions to a vote of shareholders has long been high on the wish list of many CEOs.

In recent years, the U.S. Securities and Exchange Commission (SEC) has struck down more and more shareholder resolutions on the grounds they represent shareholder intrusion into "ordinary company business."

This year, it became clear that the issue was coming to a head, as the SEC held public "round table" discussions on this and related issues. Now the regulatory agency has published drafts of new rules, soliciting public comment. While the proposed rules don't directly challenge the right to come up with advisory shareholder resolutions, they present a number of "concepts" for comment that pose real potential for future SEC action to limit or eliminate them.

Why does this matter? Well, a look back at the Kimberly-Clark situation can help make things clear. A number of environmental organizations confronted Kimberly-Clark on the issue of logging rainforests in British Columbia and elsewhere, but progress was slow until a coalition of investors—mutual funds, including mine, and institutions that hold Kimberly-Clark's stock in their portfolios—became involved.

As owners, we initiated discussions with the company's management on this key issue. What really got the company's attention was the formal filing of shareholder resolutions.

One of the world's biggest wood buyers has reduced demand for wood from sensitive rainforests, increased demand for wood from responsibly managed forests, and sent the market a message about demand for recycled pulp as well.

The implications for climate change, as well as for the Spirit Bears, are enormous. This is how big change happens, and this is why so many U.S. investors focused their attention last summer on telling the SEC that their right to propose shareholder resolutions matters.

$\mathcal{H}$ell no,
we won't invest

In general, I'm against war. Perhaps this comes from being the daughter of a man who spent his childhood in hiding and his young teen years fighting "The Dictator," as he put it. I'm not sure. Certainly, World War II was a just war, if there is such a thing. My father believed it was. But that didn't stop the nightmares he developed during the last 10 years of his life.

When Yugoslavia broke into parts, largely because of religious differences but also due to ethnic ones, minority populations were rounded up and shot. It was for this reason that the United Nations sent in troops. In 1994, the U.N. ran air strikes in Bosnia to protect minorities. The jets flew out of Naples, Italy, where my father's sister still lived. She called, crying. It had been almost 45 years since she had heard bombers overhead, but she was scared.

My father took her call and then he turned to me. "Those people in Bosnia, they don't care why the bombs are dropping. They only think about who is dropping them." That's the way it is with war. Reason is stripped; survival is all. Survivors never really survive; they just live on.

I manage money for a living. I buy stocks. But I don't buy stocks of companies that make weapons. Used as intended, bombs kill people. So do landmines, guns, and a host of other military products. They kill people. The survivors don't survive. (That's also the problem with tobacco, another product in which I don't invest.) When you come down to it, who does want wars?

You can make it hard to define weapons. Is it the trailer that has been customized to haul the load that makes the bomb? I say it is a matter of degree. But generally, it is really easy. Anyone can avoid buying stocks in the biggest, most committed weapons builders.

Unfortunately, corporations in the war business want wars. Wars stimulate the demand for their products. Irregular Times (irregulartimes.com) carries a nifty picture of the interwoven relationships among the top defense contractors. It turns out that these companies share lobbyists. In 2010, leading defense firms lobbied in tandem and were rewarded with $138 billion in federal contracts. That is sort of discouraging. I lobbied for community development funds. We got $227 million.

There are a lot of good reasons not to buy shares in weapons companies. The corporate form and capitalism itself are very good if what you want is to distribute your product as cheaply as possible to as many people as possible. Distributing weapons cheaply and widely doesn't work for me. If we need weapons, I'd prefer our government make them and keep them for our national security. If we contract with these firms instead of doing it ourselves, profit margins come into play. General Dynamics' gross profit margin is 20 percent. Raytheon's is 20.6 percent. So it feels to me as though we pay 20 percent more than necessary for weapons.

Now, you may say the federal government is too inefficient to do anything as well as General Dynamics or Raytheon, but why do we pay our top generals some $200,000 a year while the CEO of General Dynamics got $13.7 million in total compensation last year? I don't know. The men and women at the helm of our armed forces seem like they are more important to national security than a b-school grad who stuck it out long enough to get the corner office.

People who avoid weapons in their stock portfolios define weapons differently. Some church groups don't buy stock in firms that produce weapons of mass destruction. Norway's Oil Trust refuses to invest in cluster munitions manufacturers. Probably reasons vary as well. Many avoid weapons because they abhor war. Others, like the Norwegian government, avoid investments that conflict with the highest aspirations of the country.

Maybe my arguments don't carry water. But when I read that more of our soldiers have committed suicide after returning from Iraq and Afghanistan than have died there, it comforts me to know I didn't directly benefit from the hell they went through.

The investor's dilemma

A campaign is underway on American college campuses. Nationwide, students are lobbying university trustees to divest endowment funds of companies that produce fossil fuels. These students no longer want stocks and bonds in the coal, oil, and natural gas industries to fund their schools. Meanwhile, the trustees are responding in the same way as companies in South Africa did during the time of apartheid: It is too big a segment of our economy. A company does not care who owns stock. You use their products, don't you?

But proponents of fossil fuel divestment are not standing down. Theirs is not a pragmatic position; it is a moral one. They argue that we cannot sell the future of the planet for a few more years of profit. To destroy life as we know it because we are fond of electricity or cars is immoral. To profit from the destruction of life as we know it is immoral. It is an argument I understand.

The website data360.org and the Responsible Endowments Coalition tell us we already have, in the hands of the corporations that provide fossil fuels, five times more in known reserves than climate scientists say is safe to burn. Yikes! Five times more fossil fuels than the planet we love and need can survive? What are we thinking?

I've worked in the field of responsible investing for decades. During that time, it was difficult to find fossil fuel companies to buy. After all, responsible investors put people and the planet first and fossil fuel extraction companies have an awful lot of accidents at worksites and create an awful lot of air and groundwater pollution. When we looked at companies one by one, we found few to invest in.

As a result, it has always been an under-represented sector of the portfolio, but that's what responsible investing is: Aspirational.

This is new, though; this is a debate over complete divestment, not about finding a few "sort of okay" firms. On moral grounds, we must not benefit from companies that actively contribute to the destruction of life on Earth, the proponents of divestment say. As I write, the oil and gas producer Exxon Mobil is the largest company in the Standard & Poors 500 index, and the energy sector represents 10.58 percent of the index. That's a big nut to work around.

It is worth remembering that when I first developed the idea of an index for responsible investors, the Domini 400 Social Index (now the MSCI/KLD 400 Social Index), we were South Africa free. At that time, even though the non-citizenship of black people in that country was arguably a form of slavery, companies doing business in South Africa represented 57 percent of the S&P 500. And though I did use IBM typewriters and drink Coca-Cola back then—while both companies were doing big business in South Africa—using the products and benefiting financially from morally repugnant behavior are two different things.

I'm still not clear where this will lead. The portfolio manager in me wants a more gradual approach, but I fear that will simply not do. Here in the U.S., we took a gradual approach to stopping slavery. Rather than stopping it, we banned the importation of slaves in 1808. But banning importation didn't get us gradually out of owning slaves; we owned more slaves 40 years later. It took the Civil War and the 13th Amendment in 1865 to get us out of the slave trade. No, incrementalism doesn't seem like the answer.

I haven't finalized my thinking on the matter. In general, I like my portfolios to reflect the ideals of the average responsible or ethical investor. But with each college divestment, the norm is become more fossil fuel free. And with each passing day, the urgency of climate change is becoming more apparent.

"That's a big nut to work around."

On the corporate frontline

W hen I met Father Seamus Finn almost 20 years ago, he held up a baseball and grinned at me. "What do you think about baseball, Amy? Is it as sweet as apple pie?" I hadn't a clue what he was getting at, but it didn't take long. "Ever see them made? I have."

For me, it was the opening salvo of the sweatshop debate. I used to sew my best clothes myself. But somewhere along about 1975, I found I could buy things that were just fine for me at less than I could make them. Even when I valued my time at zero, stores could underprice me! I started buying dresses at low-cost chain stores. I wasn't alone. People throughout developed countries discovered they were able to buy more and more low-cost stuff, which they believed meant they were living better lives. We never looked back at the whole chain of production to see that our marvelous bargains were the cause of human hardship beyond description.

Seamus was outraged that an American icon, the baseball, was being made in the heat of inland Haiti inside the crummiest of tin-roofed shacks by workers who were frequently crippled by their jobs. It is grueling work, since baseballs are stuffed with thread wound by hand into the shape of a ball. Seamus wanted to get together human rights groups, companies, investors, and people of faith so we could come to a win-win way to manufacture baseballs and other products. But companies didn't want to participate. What did he do? He filed a shareholder resolution.

In the United States, a person owning at least $2,000 worth of a company's stock for more than two years can, according to the regulations, raise an issue to which the board of the company must respond. Shareholder resolutions have been the tool of choice for concerned persons, foundations, church groups, unions, and others for many years. Looking at the sweatshop issue shows how adaptable and helpful shareholder resolutions can be.

When I survey shareholders in my own socially responsible investment company, asking them what they most want to avoid, the answer comes back, "sweatshops." But it's difficult to steer clear of all sweatshops as an investor, just as it is as a consumer. We must spend time figuring out which companies involved with sweatshops are the most inappropriate holdings for a responsible social investor.

At first, we wanted companies to sign codes of conduct for sourcing goods. After all, companies that signed such codes should have better labor practices than others. But we soon learned that the companies buying parts or finished goods from other sources didn't put much effort into ensuring the sourcing codes were followed. Then we asked that there be audits. Next, we asked for third-party audits. After that, we asked for disclosure regarding actions taken by the purchasing company when violations were found. And so forth.

Today, thanks to almost two decades of shareholder resolutions, we see improvements in the employment conditions and lives of voiceless workers around the world. We are still a long way from knowing the true cost of acquiring a new baseball, or bargain clothing, but shareholder activism has given civil society the tools to learn. Without it, we would continue to think we were smart to buy low-cost T-shirts; with it, we know we are oppressors unless that T-shirt manufacturer specifically tells us otherwise.

$\mathcal{A}$ more socially responsible strategy

Barack Obama has taken office at a critical time in U.S. history. We're fighting two wars and facing what the new U.S. President and others have called the biggest financial crisis since the Great Depression. Stock markets have collapsed more than 50 percent from peak to trough in most parts of the world. But the meltdown began in the U.S., and at least part of the solution must come from here. Below are some of my ideas, drawn from years as a student of the financial markets and as a socially responsible investor, about how to return some sanity to financial markets.

Re-regulate

There's a difference between making money and stealing it. Recent events, like the uncovering of what I view as criminally sloppy ratings of credit default swaps (financial mechanisms designed to transfer the risk of default on certain types of securities), have underlined that difference. The tide of financial deregulation that began 30 years ago must be reversed. More open and transparent reporting by companies and more aggressive enforcement of existing regulations are step one.

Rein in private equity and hedge funds

Hedge funds and private equity funds are largely unregulated, and their managers can do a variety of things that ordinary investors can't—like borrow 20 times as much capital as they raise. Though they maneuver in ways that are frequently risky and lacking in transparency, fund managers have been allowed free rein because they cater to supposedly sophisticated investors with high net worth. But "sophisticated" investors don't always exercise good judgment.

The U.S. Securities and Exchange Commission (SEC) has a mandate to protect investors, but in this case it has walked away from any responsibility toward the ultimate investors, who include pension fund beneficiaries and other members of the general public. The SEC also has a mandate to protect the general public from market abuses. It isn't particularly relevant to those who were harmed by the actions of hedge funds and private equity funds that these funds' investors were sophisticated. Those of us who were innocent bystanders need greater protection from such "sophistication." The SEC must develop reporting mandates, capital requirements, and strict governance standards, including independent directorships, for hedge funds and private equity funds.

Deter speculators
Only when speculators are driven from the market will real investors dare enter: Investors interested in the earnings and long-term prospects of companies, not in what their stocks will do in the next few days or weeks.

To help deter speculation, one easy first step would be to reinstate the uptick rule, which allows an investor to sell a stock short only when its price is rising. (Short selling is a practice through which an investor makes money if the price of a stock goes down.) The rule was in force for decades and prevented short-sellers from pushing stock prices down for profit. The uptick rule was reversed in July 2007, leading to a huge jump in this form of speculation. The President could also tax gains made from short-term stock trading at an extremely high rate, eliminating this damaging way of operating by making it unprofitable, or he could end the practice of announcing each quarter's expected earnings. The earnings guidance game reinforces the emphasis on short-term profit that has done so much to unbalance the markets and the economy.

Emphasize the beneficiary
"Fiduciary responsibility" has been a familiar excuse for money managers and speculators who seek the greatest profits for their clients without considering that those clients need a clean planet and a just society if they're to enjoy those profits.

President Obama should start in two ways. First, he should direct the Financial Accounting Standards Board, which regulates accountants in the U.S., to review its standards for what information is "material." The current system allows most environmental and social risks to go unreported, enabling fiduciaries to ignore them. Second, Obama should revisit the Employee Retirement Income Security Act (ERISA), which governs a wide range of employee benefit plans. He should ensure that the standards guiding ERISA fiduciaries take into account the overall well-being of the beneficiary.

*W*hat the world needs now

One thing that makes investing so much fun is all the learning it allows. A curious mind is always picking up new things to study. I have gotten much better at recognizing birds and wildflowers as life goes on. However, I doubt I would have learned much about the myriad component parts that go into making a new industry function were I not an investor.

There was a time when industries grew more slowly and I could learn by experience. I could see the punch cards that created instructions that the company would execute. I saw that give way to early home computers that you would type your DOS instructions into, which allowed me to understand the mind, so to speak, of the computer. There were Yellow Pages sold in paper books with the address of whatever you were looking for.

And then came AOL, or America Online, which had been an internal club of sorts, and a million new users hopped aboard the Internet and pushed web development, which pushed search engines, which pushed social sites, which pushed feedback loops, and so on. I could sort of keep up with the logic as it unfolded.

Now, however, the speed of progress, combined with the many interesting developments in the world, force me to move beyond personal experience to book learning. That's because I'm an old-fashioned investor. Today there is a newfangled sort of investment advisor that I don't fully understand. They buy dozens of mutual funds for a single client and try to balance them in a way that might be sensible but strikes me as no fun at all.

What I like is to find a few good companies, understand what they do and whether it matters, and invest in them. And when I say "invest," I mean it: buy and watch, hopefully for years. When you do that, you want to feel that the company is the right answer for what the world wants or needs today. Since I am a socially responsible investor, I'm more interested in what it needs.

This takes me back to learning. Did you realize that the World Health Organization has identified the diseases most urgently needing treatment if we are to save the most lives? According to the WHO, HIV/AIDS, tuberculosis, malaria, and neglected tropical diseases have a serious impact on health outcomes in every region of the world. What does it take to slow those diseases?

The deeper you dig, the more angles you find. It starts with education. The local population has to know the early symptoms of the disease and seek to prevent it. Prevention won't always work, so there must be a way to test for it. And the testing has to be done without sending results in a van to a testing center, since the roads might be bad. The treatments have to be simple, and the medicine has to be properly taken. While it's important to find the company with the best drug treatment, that's not the only factor to look at as an investor.

~~~~~~~~~~~~~~~~

Some people invest by the numbers alone. If, in their opinion, the stock is undervalued, they don't really care what the company does. But even if I felt okay about owning stock in companies that do terrible things to make money, that sort of investing bores me. For me, the numbers come last. After I find a solution that I want to share in, then I try to determine whether the stock is worth the price. That way, I don't lose out on the most interesting part: learning.

~~~~~~~~~~~~~~~~

There are other solutions that I've sought. Each has taken me down fascinating corridors of learning. For instance, you can't get solar energy to a grid without the right technology. Online banking is denied to most poor people because they are not on the Internet, but camera phones can be used to do the job. Most cancers "shapeshift" to avoid death by drugs, but lots of solutions seem to hold hope. Organics are hard to find when you shop for groceries at inner-city convenience stores or live in many rural areas, but organic packaged foods make it possible to get these products to consumers who were once shut out.

Investing can be a lot of fun. Thinking about the world you would like to see and finding ways to get from here to there are really very interesting. And when your investments succeed, you feel real pride in the time you took to find them.

For me, the numbers come last.

Thoughts on People, The Planet & Profit

Amy Domini is founder and chair of Domini Impact Investments. Widely recognized as the leading voice for socially responsible investing, *Time* magazine named Ms. Domini to its Time 100 list of the world's most influential people. Other awards include the Clinton Global Initiative citation for innovation and finance, an honorary Doctor of Business Administration degree from Northeastern College of Law, an honorary Doctor of Laws degree from Flagler College, and an honorary Doctor of Humane Letters from Yale University's Berkeley Divinity School. Ms. Domini has also been named to *Directorship* magazine's Directorship 100, the magazine's listing of the most influential people on corporate governance and in the boardroom, and *Barron's* selected her as one of the 30 most influential people in the mutual fund business.

Active in her community, Ms. Domini is a board member for the Center for Responsible Lending. She is also a past board member of the Church Pension Fund of the Episcopal Church in America; the National Association of Community Development Loan Funds, an organization whose members work to create funds for grassroots economic development loans; and the Interfaith Center on Corporate Responsibility, the major sponsor of shareholder actions. A frequent guest commentator, Ms. Domini has appeared on CNBC's Talking Stocks and various other radio and television shows.

In addition to a BA in international and comparative studies from Boston University, Ms. Domini has also earned the CFA designation.

Ms. Domini lives in Cambridge, Massachusetts with her husband and gray cat. In her free time, she enjoys teaching her five grandchildren how to garden.

Made in United States
North Haven, CT
11 December 2021

12389472R00089